Marco
Polo

A Life From Beginning to End

*(The Amazing Explorer Who Discovered New
Worlds and Changed History Forever)*

Frederick Meyerson

Published By **Andrew Zen**

Frederick Meyerson

Marco Polo: A Life From Beginning to End (The Amazing Explorer Who Discovered New Worlds and Changed History Forever)

ISBN   978-1-990373-82-4

No part of this guidebook shall be reproduced in any form without permission in writing from the publisher except in the case of brief quotations embodied in critical articles or reviews.

Legal & Disclaimer

The information contained in this book is not designed to replace or take the place of any form of medicine or professional medical advice. The information in this book has been provided for educational & entertainment purposes only.

The information contained in this book has been compiled from sources deemed reliable, and it is accurate to the best of the Author's knowledge; however, the Author cannot guarantee its accuracy and validity and cannot be held liable for any errors or omissions. Changes are periodically made to this book. You must consult your doctor or get professional medical advice before using any of the suggested remedies, techniques, or information in this book.

Table Of Contents

Chapter 1: A Boy In Venice

YOUNG MARCO POLO gazed at the vast blue ocean from a high windows in his house in Venice. In the distance beyond his home in the Gulf of Venice he saw the wide Adriatic filled with vessels carrying goods. In the midst of it all the man saw one of the galleys used in war with a crew of a hundred or so oars racing quickly over the sea to guard the harbor from enemy attack and the cargo vessels that were rich from the ravagers.

When he sat looking at the sea, young Marco thought about his dreams. He envisioned the day he could embark on a voyage to distant ports on Sicily as well as Greece. He imagined exploring the city of Constantinople in which his uncle and father owned docks and structures. He envisioned the enigmatic places to which the Crusaders went. It is possible that he too will one day travel to these distant locations. It is also possible that he will be able to see one day the amazing marvels of the globe.

In awe, he sat at the ocean and dreamed of the immense world behind. Through his entire life, he resided in the city of Venice. However, to this port, ships came from many locations and he'd read about the world that were beyond. The man had also heard stories about a lands that are still undiscovered that was full of wonders and mysteries.

Some believed that just beyond the frontier of the Caucasus the vast expanse of land which stretched for miles. They also claimed that nobody had explored this area to the east because the path was blocked by the Tartar hoards.

Young Marco was wondering if that was the realm that his father or uncle went. A trip like this was, in his opinion, going to require a long time. What if his uncle and father been absent for a while? It's been longer. It is certain that soon, someday the time comes, they will be back. He hoped one of the boats was visible approaching the port of Venice would be bringing them back home. He wanted to see them return.

Marco aged six at the time the father of his son Nicolo along with his father Maffeo married and had never been married, left Venice's port Venice carrying a significant cargo of goods. They had hoped to disappear just a year or so and left little Marco with the grandparents of the mother of his child had passed away as a baby. However, after a number of years gone by and the Polos didn't return and the family was worried that Nicolo and Maffeo had disappeared. Marco was, however, not one to be let go of the possibility of a return. He was certain that one day, his uncle and father returned. When he was just six years old, the uncle and father quit; he is now 15 years old. At the time they left, he was an infant. He felt strong and grew.

One day in Marco's fifteenth birthday, the way he'd hoped for to see, a ship sailing into the port of Venice returned his uncle and father. They had been away for over nine years, and finally returned home to their family.

The evening was a celebration held at the Polo home in order to welcome back the city of Venice The two brothers that had travelled across the country and had been absent for all of a year. The guests at the dinner included Venetian nobles, former family and close friends and masters of the merchants guild. The young Marco stood proudly with his father.

Once the food was finished and the table cleaned, Marco's parents and uncle made the large-scale chart that was laid out and placed on the table to look at.

"This will help us explain our long journey," explained Nicolo. "With this map which we ourselves have drawn, we will try to trace our route and tell you how it happened that we finally arrived at the lands of the Tartars."

The guests around the table stared at one another. They were frightened at their faces because they all knew they Tartars were a strong and fighting race. Just fifty years ago, their armies crossed the Danube. Even at this time, the terrible Tartars were still an existential threat to the peace in Europe. Which lands had been conquered by them! Did their conquests last forever!

"Yes," repeated Nicolo boldly. "We have been to the land of the Tartars."

"It is true," said the brother Maffeo. "We have not only been to the land of the Tartars, but we have seen their emperor Kublai Khan and are now returned as his personal envoys."

The terror in the guests' eyes changed to amazement. Everyone was silent. They were all eager to learn the story Nicolo and Maffeo would be sharing.

While he was putting his finger on the map, Nicolo tracked the route of their boat. "Nine years ago, in the year 1260," the man said, "we sailed from the Gulf of Venice." After that, he described how upon reaching safely in Constantinople where they discovered the warehouses and ships filled with a variety of goods. Everything was in perfect state and, as the presence of their ships in Constantinople was not required in a hurry the group decided to look into potential trade opportunities in some of the regions around that Black Sea. To do this, they needed to travel via horses. They brought with them numerous expensive jewels that they were able to hide and transport easily. They hoped to use these gems to exchange them.

When they rode on horseback, across the shores of Black Sea they reached the camp that was occupied by one of the Tartar generals. The chief was a generous prince who respected the culture of his country. He immediately received the Polo brothers and greeted their guests with the same respect given to ambassadors. The Polo brothers stayed for the whole year in the company of Tartar Prince. Tartar Prince. They learned to communicate in the Mongolian dialect that was spoken by the Tartars.

They also discovered that there were countries in which they had to go were at war with each other This meant that they had to undertake an extended deviation. The detour took them to the east. They traversed over the Volga River and then spent 17 days traveling across a barren stretch of desert. Then they retreated into the realm of Persia.

This was the long distance was the one Marco's father Nicolo sketched out across the map in front of him. After that, pointing out a specific location, he said that it was the location within Persia in which they were able to meet an important ambassador. The ambassador was heading to meet the Khan Tartars living in the Far Eastern lands.

The ambassador was very satisfied with their Polo brothers. They were adroit and amiable. They could speak with one another in the Mongolian tongue. Soon, the ambassador proposed to have the Polo brothers join him at the Kublai Khan's court. Kublai Khan. The ambassador was sure that his brothers will be enthralled by the amazing landscape of the land is known as Cathay. It was his belief that as the Khan has never met any indigenous people from Europe He would be delighted to welcome them into his palace. This Nicolo described to the guests sitting around the table. With his fingers, he meticulously traced their lengthy route to the court of Khan Kublai located in distant Cathay.

"From Persia we travelled in the direction of east. We traveled on many roads traversed many countries. We traveled over high mountains, as well as vast areas of desert. However, all of these things don't matter. It is important that finally, after more than a year's travel we arrived at the court of the legendary Kublai Khan.

We were welcomed as kingly guests. At this point, we became fluent in the Mongolian dialect and we could converse with him without hesitation. It was amazing how many things he was interested in knowing! He asked a myriad of questions because we were among the first visitors that came from Europe to whom he'd encountered. We were asked questions about the countries through which we travelled and was interested in the different kingdoms that existed in Europe and the way they were managed. He was fascinated by every aspect. He wanted to know more about our faith. We provided all of the information the man inquired about. He was fascinated by the Pope, so he wanted us to teach him about the Christian faith."

The Polo brothers explained to Khan that the Christian religion was different from religious traditions of the Orient and that they believed Christianity is superior to all other religions.

The Khan was astonished to find the Polo brothers to have a great sense and the latest information. After consulting with his Ministers The Khan chose to hire as his ambassadors Pope Francis. Pope.

Then Maffeo said: "Here are the letters that the Khan wrote for the Pope. The letters ask the Pope to give to Cathay 100 educated men, fully familiar with the fundamentals of Christianity and the seven art forms that form the basis of our society. Many times, we have told the Khan that the seven arts are rhetoric and logic, as well as grammar, music, astronomy, math, and geometrical thinking. The Khan wants to see these hundred knowledgeable men be invited to Cathay to be his guests. In Cathay the Khan would like them to impart to the scholars of his court what they are aware of. In the end, if the hundred or so men prove that the faith of Christ is superior to other faiths, the Khan said that he as well as all those under his authority were to turn into Christians."

The moment these words were said The Polo brothers took out the extravagant gifts that Kublai Khan was sending to the Pope. The gifts were displayed before their stunned guests.

"And here," said Nicolo pulling the collar off of his jacket, "here is the golden tablet that was given to us by Khan. It is written in Mongolian language, and it bears that of an Emperor. Everywhere we traveled within Cathay the golden talisman was a guarantee for us everything that was essential. There was only one thing to ask."

He held the gold symbol for the world to see. It was nearly equal to the length of his hand but was not so wide. The tag made of pure gold was tied on his neck with the silken cord. Young Marco as he sat next to his father was able to see the exquisite Mongolian engravings on the golden emblem of power. It was an odd script that was written in a language which was utterly foreign to me.

Nicolo then opened the letter to the Pope that he received come from the Khan and showed the seal of the Khan's imprint with royal vermilion.

After a few minutes of silence, one noble at the table said "You are away in the sea which means you couldn't be aware of the tragic report. A few months ago the pope we revered, Clement IV, passed away. The cardinals are currently in the midst of a journey towards Rome."

"This is indeed sad news," told Nicolo. "For this moment we'll need to wait until a new

Pope has been appointed. Khan has a goal to bring in one hundred experienced men of Europe."

In the evening, after guests left the young Marco requested to revisit the Khan's golden tablet that let his soldiers to ask the things they would need during their travels. That was an amazing item. He studied it with a keen eye. The eyes of his were glistening in amazement.

"How long, Father, does it take to elect a new pope in Rome?" I asked Marco.

"Not long," replied his father.

"Then you will be returning to the Khan in Cathay?"

"Yes, we have promised faithfully that we shall return."

Young Marco turned his attention to his father. "When you sail again," the boy said in a confident voice, "then I will sail alongside you. I am ready."

"How are you ready?" asked his father.

"All the years, I've had no time to sit idle. My teachers have been training me to be merchant. They've instructed me in Persian and I am aware of the way a ship must go. I am familiar with the ropes as well as the sails. I'm able to study a chart as well as measure wind speed. And I can steer using the night sky and with compass throughout the daytime. Additionally, I have an adequate background in arithmetic, geography and the history."

"Good," said his father. He was delighted by Marco as well as his accomplishments and his enthusiasm and youthfulness. Also, he was pleased by his appearance. In front of him was a growing youthful man of medium height and wide shoulders. His head, well-set, was adorned with dark, curly hair. His eyes were dark brown big and sparkled. The lips of his were perfectly made, his chin was sturdy and his nose perfectly designed. His eyebrows were straight and overall there was around the man an intelligence radiating out of his face. Nicolo Polo looked over at his son with a smile and smiled.

"You have grown, you are strong," the man declared. "Yes, this time you shall go with us to the court of Kublai Khan."

It was a fantastic day. What a beautiful day. However, Marco's happiness was no limits.

The night that young Marco was asleep, the young Marco dreamed of distant lands and strange race of people. The dreamer envisioned oriental sights, of wonders and splendour.

He awoke up early on the following day. He could see the edge of the sun rising over and the eastern horizon that spanned the bay. What was the distance to east of the sun? How far to the east was Cathay?

Very soon the man would travel toward the east, heading towards that enchanting land of Cathay. Cathay was the destination of the heart's dream.

Chapter 2: No Scholars For Cathay

While the POLO brothers and the young Marco were waiting at Venice There were problems with the Italian government in Rome. The cardinals' council was unable to agree on a successor for the Pope who died. The usual timeframe is some days or weeks before a decision is made. In 1269, many months had passed, and the cardinals were unable to make a decision on who they believed was suitable for this prestigious post.

"We need to be patient. It is imperative to wait" told Marco's father. "And as we wait, make sure we use the time wisely. Prepare ourselves for the journey to be long."

Marco joined in with enthusiasm to every detail of their plans. He was overwhelmed by anticipation of the trip. Then he requested his parents and uncles to instruct him in the Mongolian dialect, as they realized it was a huge advantages to him being capable of speaking with Tartars using their language. Lessons were soon started and Marco was able to learn quickly and effortlessly.

He was also keen to know all could be learned about the countries of the Orient where his uncle and father had recently returned. In these nations, only a few were recognized within Europe. Marco was constantly asking questions, and the more senior Polos explained everything they had learned.

They explained to him why they are the first people to enter the mysterious East.

"It is known that in ancient times," Nicolo told his nephew, "there was a trade route that ran from Orient across to the Holy Land and on to Rome. Merchants from the past trade in silks and spices coming via the East. However, shortly after the fall of the Roman Empire, Rome the trade route shut down. In the decades that followed, there was there was no effort made to connect to the East. The mountains of the high Caucasus as well as the Ural Mountains, and the dense Russian forests created an unnatural barrier. However, it is interesting to note that the Tartar victories have made it possible. The Tartars have carved roads through forests. They are able to bridge wild rivers, and they have pierced the mountains of sand. In fact, it was due to the military roads that you uncle and me could reach Cathay."

"It is all so interesting but so confusing," explained Marco. "Here here at home, we can be convinced in the Tartars are a ferocious heathen race that has none mercy towards their foes. They pillage, they kill. But you say that they've treated your very well and with great care. You also say they have learned and that the princes of their kingdom are very well-mannered! In reality, this is extremely difficult to comprehend."

"They treated us with great consideration," declared his father. "When you return to their realms and go through their lands that they have conquered it will be interesting to learn about their fascinating history as well as the sudden ascendance to power. It will be a universe that's entirely different from the one that you are familiar with."

Then Nicolo was asking his son: "Do you know why the people of Europe refer to these people as Tartars while in actual fact they're Mongols who hail from Mongolia in the northern part of Cathay? The reason is that tartaros in Greek is a reference to hell. The first time these army units made their way through the mountains and fought with the utmost brutality, they were believed to look like devils. Without a name to refer to them, people in Europe were able to call them "men of hell' or Tartars. We now know they are from Mongolia."

Young Marco was keen to witness this group of "men from hell" and make a decision on his own. Did they really have such a fierce stance? It was it even risky for you to be traveling with them? Would Kublai Khan's golden tablets Kublai Khan fully protect them during this lengthy trip? How soon can they get started? What were the latest developments about Rome? Will the deadlock between cardinals last forever?

The whole year was gone and there was no pope appointed. A half year was passed, but there was no pope.

The Polo brothers became annoyed. They were aware that the powerful Khan will not be thrilled at this delay. They worried that the Khan may conclude they'd broken their promises to him and they were not even an plans to return to his homeland. Since they were the Polos were the only people from Europe whom the Khan was ever acquainted with He could, as a result of this failure, conclude that all people who come from Europe violate their vows in a snap.

No. The two could not stay for much longer. Therefore, they decided to bring all the things they would need to travel with and begin plans for their departure. However, they remained uneasy. In order to reach Kublai Khan and without the hundred of the learned and educated men was his dream to have could be an ineffective way of completing their goal. However, not arriving even if they did was also undesirable. They finally decided to delay their arrival until the full two years had passed after the demise of the Pope Clement.

After two years gone by, they were determined not to delay an additional day. So, after saying goodbye to everybody, they ascended their vessel, set anchor and raised the sails. It was time to begin the journey. The bow was bobbing to the east.

Marco was sitting in the bow of the ship. He was content. He gazed out over the sea in blue. He occasionally glanced back to the Venice city. Venice with the hundred islands that surround it as well as its slender canals, and the arched bridges. The city was all he knew thoroughly. But from in the East elusive areas he didn't know about.

The bow was pounding against the turbulent water, and, with every pound, it sprayed salty water into the air. Fresh air hung in the air. The sky was wide. The blue sea continued to stretch until the eyes of his friend could see.

Finally, after two years of waiting they set out on their way. Marco was 15 years old when his parents and uncle came back to the East. He was now 17. And he was tall, and powerful.

A slight breeze carried the boats along. They navigated through the night using the help of stars in the daytime they used compasses and their charts. Sometimes they stopped in a Mediterranean port for fresh water as well as food. They also docked at times to take off the items. They traversed many scattered Greek islands before they reached the coast of Syria. The coast was near the territory of Jerusalem. Then, along the coast, they discovered the harbor of Acre, the city. Acre. Acre was the city that was the site of a capture from Richard I and his brave fighting knights.

When they slowly sailed into the harbor, Marco noticed that many of the ships, who were recognizing the pennants and flags that were flying from Venice and were offering signals to the other vessels. Then a rowboat sailed near their ship and they yelled out: "Messages have arrived from Rome! A pope has been selected!"

The lords and high-ranking officials from the city gathered at the wharf waiting to welcome them. The crowd was ablaze. The letters for the Polo brothers were sent via rapid galley. They were signed by newly elected pope Gregory X, who ordered the envoys promptly to Rome. To make this trip, the speedy war-galley carrying the documents sat in wait.

The Polos were not thrilled with this return, after making an excellent start to the long voyage, they were determined to see the Pope follow the advice of Khan and dispatch 100 of the most educated men towards the East. So, following the instructions of the sailors of their ship to take the vessel and its contents to Constantinople and then took off for the speedy war galley. It departed immediately. It sped swiftly away from the harbor.

The galley was run by 100 slaves who wailed and groaned as they put their hands on the long the oars. They were surrounded by soldiers with whips. Another hundred slaves sat on decks, ready to ease the tired from their work. The prow was sharp and split the water from front to back and a path of foam was left. In the event of favorable winds and the sails raised it appeared to Marco that they were flying across the waters surface. Then, when the sun went down, and darkness engulfed them at night, the slaves were in the helm, singing in the thumping strokes of rowers.

This way, they ran across the ocean. After a few days gone by, they finally reached the destination.

Then, in Rome, Gregory X received the gifts without a any delay. He wrote several letters to Khan, and requested the Polos with delivering elegant gifts made from crystal and gold. However, instead of the 100 scholars that Khan Khan requested to receive, the Pope requested two priests to join the Khan. "These brothers," he declared, "are men of letters and science as well as being theologians of a high caliber. They hold my power to ordain priests, consecrate bishops and grant absolution. They can accomplish anything that a hundred people can achieve." He also offered them a warm welcome for their lengthy journey before he removed them from the audience in the hall.

Again, the Polos began to move east. With two novice friars, who were never outside of Rome and returned to the coastline of Syria. The group of five purchased good pack horses and set off towards the country of Armenia. At night, they would sleep out in the open, and other evenings they stayed in lodging.

They had stayed in their homes for long distances when they received the news of a terrible fate. The sultan from Babylonia was advancing on Armenia with an army of great size and the army was already with its destruction work. Two friars were horrified of this news, and concerned for their safety and their own, decided they could be unable to continue.

"But the journey has hardly begun," said Nicolo.

"For us it has now ended," said one friar.

"The Khan waits for you. He's keen to find out more about Christianity. Do you not commitment to share the gospel that Jesus Christ taught? Christ?"

However, the sanctuary of a monastery have made friars afraid of the outside world and so they debated in this manner and that. "Let the infidels come to Rome," they eventually stated.

Then they gave to the Polos the letters the Pope handed the Polos to deliver to Khan. Khan. Turning their horses they headed back towards the shores of Syria at the fastest speed possible.

The three Polos went on with their travels. They travelled during the day and then retreated to their beds during the night. Then they found themselves in the lands and away from the shores the Mediterranean which touched all the nations in Europe. Then they entered the obscure lands in the East.

The older Polos had ridden through these lands in the east prior to. However, to the young Marco these new lands were new. As riding along, his sharp eyes caught many sights which fascinated the young man. There were strange birds, and bizarre animal species. He observed strange customs, and heard stories that were a bit spooky. All things that were interesting and new was noted by him.

In his pocket on his coat, young Marco carried notepads. He kept a record of every thing he observed, and every thing he discovered. He recorded the names of cities and nations by which they traveled. He also wrote down the other information were heard along the way and that he didn't wish to forget.

On his journey, He filled numerous sheets filled with notes. It was from those notes that, years later, he was in a position to write an entire description of his trip. The travel journal he wrote is still the most memorable trip ever documented.

Chapter 3: Fountains Of Oil

The first countries through which the Polos traversed included Armenia as well as Turkey. These were the two most westernmost provinces within the Khan's massive empire. While riding by horseback, they traveled across fair pastures in which shepherds cared for their livestock. As they arrived at an area, they stopped for a moment to drink a refreshing drink and talk to the locals. Marco was especially fascinated by watching craftsmen in their jobs. He watched how rug weaver washed and dyed their wools, and also how they made their stunning rug. Metalworkers made vessels, trays and jewellery made of silver and brass. He watched the potters working their workstations and saw the woodworkers creating intricate designs for furniture and screens. These things intrigued him. Then his uncle and father having seen the same thing previously, were made to push him forward. The road ahead was long and they couldn't stay.

After several days of travel, they arrived in the eastern part of Turkey and, in the distance they saw a snow-capped mountain which seemed to extend to the sky. In the process of getting closer, they came across a shepherd, and Marco was able to talk to the shepherd.

"It is the Mountain of the Ark," the shepherd declared. "High on its peak, Noah's ark came to rest after the flood."

"Then that must be Mount Ararat?"

"We call it simply the Mountain of the Ark," told the shepherd. "And from the high slopes of this mountain descended into this valley all living things to repopulate the world devastated by the flood."

The shepherd was a friend and informed them of various things. He was, however, fascinated. He was interested in knowing who they were as well as where they would be going.

"We are Venetians and we are going eastward," Marco said. Marco, "into the land of Persia. Further. Tell me, dear your friend, which land is towards from the North?"

"To the north lies Georgia which is the country where the flowing fountain flows. Within this region," continued the shepherd, "there is a fountain where water flows. It is not the water of the world, but rather a dark, oily liquid. People do not consume the oil as food instead, it is used as an unguent to treatment of skin irritations for cattle and humans and for various other ailments; it also helps in burning. Many people travel from far away to purchase the oil. This fountain is so plentiful that camels come daily and take great containers filled with the mysterious substance."

Marco's uncle and father were both smiling at the story of the shepherd. They knew for certain that there was no water fountain was ever found. They disagreed against the shepherd. They declared that they knew that water was the only thing to bubble out of the earth. The shepherd was insistent that his tale was real. He was acquainted with people who had witnessed this fountain and who had used its oil to ignite their lamps.

As unbelievable as the story seemed to Marco however, he still not recorded the story just as he had heard the story.

The Polos continued to travel to the point of coming to the country of Persia. The entire country was destroyed by the battle. The Tartars invaded Persia and

Persians had lost a lengthy and futile struggle against the invaders.

In the evening, while traveling through the country of Persia The Polos arrived at a city known as Saba. There they stayed the evening. They also explored the tombs of three Magi and their families, who back in the old times, had traveled to Bethlehem. They inquired about the King's from long ago however, the locals could not tell them any information. They did say, however, that the priests in the castle of fire worshippers in which they were traveling through, might be able to inform them.

After a long journey, after a long journey, the Polos arrived at the castle of fire worshipers where they stayed as guests. The castle's priests claimed that the reason that they worshipped the fire was due to they were three Magi.

Their elder came to elaborate: "In ancient times, three kings from this area were invited to the shrine of a particular prophet who had just been born. The kings brought with them presents: myrrh, gold and frankincense. They carried these to establish whether the baby prophet was a god or a king from the earth, or even a doctor. They reasoned that if the baby takes gold, surely it is the king. If he burns the incense, then he's God. If he also takes myrrh, then he's medical doctor.

"They gave their presents and the infant was able to accept the gifts in all three. It was a bit confusing for the Magi yet they kneeled in worship and praised him as they prepared to leave, the child handed them a tiny sealed box. They then travelled through the desert for a few days, and curious to find out what was within the box, cut the seal. The box included the stone. The children thought this was a little odd. It is possible the child was trying to ridicule the stone? What's a stone, anyway? Then they decided to throw the stone away. They dumped it in the pit next to it and immediately--a spark was created due to the rock's impact on an object--the whole pit burst into fires.

"In the bright glow of the fire, one of the kings spoke: "It is now crystal apparent for me. The stone is a symbol. The intention was to be strong as stones in the belief we got from Jesus Christ.'

"Then they took a portion of the flame from the pit of burning, and carried it back home. They put it into their temple and tended them with great care so that it would keep always in flame. The fire was considered sacred to the last day of their lives. In the generations which followed the three great rulers continued to worship the fire, and made all sacrifices for the flame. This sacred flame has throughout the years, been in flame. Today, we take extra precautions to make sure that it never cease to burn."

It was a story Polos Polos received from the mouth of a priest inside the castle of believers in the flames.

Marco was sure to have heard about the legend about the 3 Magi and the way they came to Bethlehem to pray for the Christ baby, however, Marco had not had heard about the stone Christ handed to the kings and the Holy Fire.

After two days of relaxation in the castle of flame worshippers and the Polos began their travels. They travelled for several days in fertile land with vast areas of wheat, cotton millet, barley, and many other varieties of grains. They visited rich vineyards and exquisite orchards.

It was in this region where Marco observed the oddest sheep ever. They were huge--almost two times the size of normal sheep. They also had large, long tails. The tails of these animals, weighing 30 to 40 pounds were incredibly meaty and delicious for eating. The sheep today are referred to for their fat tails.

Here, too, Marco saw many colourful birds--swift falcons with reddish breasts, turtledoves, pheasants, and black-and-white-peppered partridges with red beaks and legs. He brought them to his dad and uncle. He was incredibly interested in wildlife and birds.

In the end, leaving this land of fertile soil travelers came across a tiny salt desert along the eastern edge of Persia. It took them eight days and night to travel across the desert that was dry and barren. They had to bring enough food to feed themselves as well as food for their livestock as in this harsh desert, there was no town with no pubs or restaurants, nor did they have water. When on the eighth day, they could see the fields of fertile soil ahead and they could see that all risk was over and were content.

Chapter 4: Hashish--And "Assassins"

In the process of escaping PERSIA and coming into Afghanistan after which the Polos were transported to a rocky land where locals shared a story of a tyrant who was shrewd and strange. The countryside for a long time was terrorized by the demon. Just twenty years earlier, the dictator been killed and overthrown. There were many who were able to remember him, and even dared to talk about the violence he committed.

Marco Polo recorded the story in the manner that he and his uncle and father heard about it through the inhabitants of this region. The man in question was known as Sheik al-Jabal. The word translated refers to the Old Man from the Mountain.

In the past, a sheik from Arabia who was chief head of his tribe was forced out of his foes in Egypt. His entire tribe joined his footsteps. When they arrived in the mountainous region of Afghanistan they came across the beautiful valley the highest point, atop an edifice of rock They saw the castle fortress at Alamut. They repelled the castle and seized it with the force of.

The sheik then ordered the construction of stone walls and fortifications be constructed on both sides of the ravine in order to ensure the fortress was secure from any enemies. The beautiful valley was where the sheik created lavish gardens that included flowers, fruit trees as well as fountains and flowers. The gardens were erected by him fresh-water pools as well as a variety of tiny palaces, which filled with treasures made of silver and gold, including furniture, paintings, silk rugs and other rare items. These were all things the tribe and he had taken from caravans that passed by.

The pleasure gardens as well as palaces were complete and adorned with the luxury the sheik could think of, the sheik picked the most gorgeous young ladies of the tribe who would live in the palace. The girls he chose excelled in the art of dance, singing, and playing musical instruments. They were provided with extravagant dresses and accessories. They were looked after and supervised by matrons, who stayed in the house and rarely visited the garden.

He was known as a brutal master who ruled with an iron grip. The sheik instructed his priests to educate all kids of his clan to believe that he was primary prophetess of Mohammed and should be worshiped because he was the only one who was able to allow the dead to go to the paradise of heaven. Children believed in the priests they had and were raised to revere their sheiks with the highest respect.

In order to protect his mountain castle and maintain a watchful eye out for intruders, the sheik brought to the castle with a group of men in their teens. The sheik chose only the strongest as well as obedient, and showed determination. The young men took part in daily exercise and were instructed by their captains in order to serve as guards for the castle. In the meantime priests provided them with theological instruction, and reiterated time and again that their sheik was their ultimate ruler and that he was Mohammed's prophet Mohammed and that only he was able to grant them access to the paradise. So, everything should they be pleasing to the sheik or else they'd find that the gates to paradise locked.

The priests from this tribe were not just experts in religious matters, but were also knowledgeable about substances. The hemp plant's leaves they crafted a narcotic called hashish.

In some instances, it was the Old Man of the Mountains would demand that the substance be placed into the diet of more than a dozen youths who were instructed as guards for castles. When the youths became totally drunk and unconscious, they were taken through the valley, and then taken into the secret gardens of palaces.

After a short time, after the effects of the drug started to wear off, the males opened their eyes and were surrounded by luxury beyond what they had ever imagined. Every youth who was recuperating from the euphoria caused by the drug, discovered himself surrounded by beautiful damsels who performed soothing songs, sung and danced. Once he was completely awake, they served the delectable dishes that they served with exquisite wine. They also encouraged the man to enjoy every pleasure he wanted. These young people were filled with joy that they believed they were transported to heaven.

The extreme pleasures lasted for around five days. Then again, the youngsters were secludedly drank and towed down the mountain back towards the fortress. After they got up at night, the sheik appeared on their home and inquired to tell him where they'd been.

"Through your kind favour, your Highness, we have been allowed to visit paradise." That was the answer everyone received.

The priests who attended the events declared: "We have the assurance of the holy prophets who have spoken to us that the one who defends God and abides by his commands will be granted heaven.

Only when you're faithful and obey his commands is happiness and a paradisiacal paradise ever again be yours."

In response the moment, everyone said that they were prepared to obey the orders from their superior. They only had to be ordered by the men--and even if to go to the grave and die, they'd be happy as servants of the holy sheikh.

The Old Man of the Mountain created lists of his adversaries as well as the princes of his neighbors whom he disliked. He then sent out the youngsters whom he so strictly controlled. They carried concealed daggers. They pledged not to return until the act was completed. The ferocious young men spread terror across the nations. Due to the substance, hashish that they consumed they were called Hashishins. The name, however, was not easy to pronounce, and people living in the frightened regions identified them as"Assassins. The very first "assassins" in the world were trained by the old Man who was the mountain, who had the power of Castle Fortress.

Then, when the Tartar governor of the province learned concerning the Old Man of the Mountain and his trained assassins, he dispatched an army to these areas. They immediately laid up a siege on the castle's stronghold. However, since the castle's position located on a rocky cliff was virtually inaccessible, and was easily defendable and defended, the commander Tartar officer decided to keep the castle in a secure area to prevent unnecessary losses of his troops. Therefore, he smothered the inhabitants of Hashishin into submission. This was a gradual process but it was also a secure one. After a few years, all of the supplies in the fortress were gone and the fortress was surrounded, the defenders opened the gates and handed over their weapons. It was the time that The Old Man of the Mountain as well as his followers were slain to death by Tartar troops, and his mountain fortress was destroyed and his garden was demolished.

In the long-running siege, quite some of the drug-consuming tribe escaped the ravine's rocky slope. A few were reported to have been as having been spotted in Syria as well, while others were believed to have escaped over the mountains to take refuge in the north of India.

The entire bizarre history that the Polos learnt from their people whom they exchanged words with. The people for a long time been in fear. They were now at peace. The rule of the iron Old Man of the Mountains was finally wiped out.

BONES GUIDE THE TRAVELLER

LAVOIDING LANDSCAPE OF THE old Man of the Mountain The travelers traveled through a thriving countryside that was gorgeous and abundant in fruits as well as corn and vines. The people, however, were treacherous, and Polos were in constant danger. Polos were constantly in risk of losing their own lives.

After a further few months of travel, they arrived in the province that was known as Balashan. In the moment they arrived in this province they had entered the western part of the territory that is in the northern part of India and extends eastward until the borders of China. The province remains in the present day as among the most primitive frontiers of civilisation. Only a handful of travelers in the past Polos had ever tried to travel through this region. Marco Polo was the very first European journeyman to explore the region and record notes of his travels.

The Balashan province Balashan is a rough country with mountain ranges with sweeping peaks, fast rivers as well as deep ravines. The Polos encountered a wide variety of wild animals as well as strange creatures. Also, the inhabitants, seemed strange and wild.

This region was controlled by a prince that claimed to be the descendants of Alexander the Great due to his marriage to his daughter Darius Darius, the king of Persians. There was a claim that there was a horse breed that were derived directly from Alexander's famed horse Bucephalus. All colts were born in a special way, with the mark of the forehead.

Marco Polo was told that within the mountains were discovered precious rubies as well as the stunning blue stone known as lapis lazuli. These precious stones, which were embedded in the mountains of the highest peaks were mined exactly the same way as silver and gold. Lapis lazuli was discovered flowing in wide veins. There were silver mines as well as copper, lead and.

Marco Polo recorded that the inhabitants of the country were skilled archers, and adorned them with skins of wild animals. He was awed by the number of falcons as well as other species of birds that he could see from the skies and the huge number of wild sheep that wandered about in groups that included four, five or 600.

After leaving the province of Balashan, Marco, with his uncle and father, arrived at a wall of mountains.

Over the course of days, they would climb one mountain following another, rising upwards and upwards until finally they came to a place at which Marco believed that the nearby mountain ranges must be the highest areas in the entire world. In this place in between two ranges where they encountered an enormous lake, from where a river flowed to an immense plain that was covered in lush grass.

The Polos traveled across the lofty plain, also known as"the Pamir Plateau. In all of these days they never saw any human settlements. But they did find isolated herdersmen who were tending their animals.

A few nights ago, the Polos were sitting around the campfire, and had a conversation to a shepherd. Marco had seen numerous huge mountain sheep with horns that were twisted to perfection and twisted horns, was interested to learn more about them.

"Why are there so many skeletons and horns of these beautiful sheep lying about the countryside?" Marco asked. Marco. "You herdsmen do not kill them, do you?"

"Oh, no," replied the herdsman. "Only rarely do we kill an animal for its food. However, this region is populated with wolves who are marauding and are wolves that kill lots of their prey."

"It is a great pity," Marco said. Marco.

"No, it does not really matter," declared the herdsman. "For there are plenty of them. Additionally the bones and horns they leave behind, their bones serve us. Bowls and ladles are made using the horns of their animals. As you've probably observed as you traveled on, we are also using the horns to build corrals for our livestock."

The herdsman reached for an enormous leather bag and pulled out a few bowls and ladles in order to demonstrate the Polos. Marco was of the opinion that these tools are rather crude, however it was his belief that the herders were skilled in using the traditional the horns that they had in this manner.

The herdsman continued to speak. "We herders also collect the bones and horns scattered around of dead sheep. They create piles of them on the end of the highway. It is likely that you have seen them. This is an aid for travelers in winter months in the winter when roads are covered by snow."

While sitting by the campfire that night, Marco kept meticulous notes of what the herdsman said as well as of all the things he saw. One of the points he noted is the observation that fires at this elevation did not appear to emit the same amount of heat as those located in lower elevations. The author also penned a description of mountain sheep with horns that were twisted to the extreme, which lived in the area. He didn't know while he wrote that he was the very first person to record the journey about this animal.

After being found by modern-day explorers, they were able to identify them exactly the way Marco Polo had described them. Then, in honor of Marco Polo, they the sheep were named Ovis Poli meaning simply the sheep of Marco Polo.

As the Polos were cruising along this high tableland they could observe a few of the mountains covered in snow of the imposing Himalayas. The peaks that are the highest on earth--are above twenty-five thousand feet. Also, Marco said that no bird were seen at the summits.

Then, after 12 days, they reached the top of the plateau's green and for the next forty days they continued their journey towards Cathay traversing mountains and valleys, passing through one range after another. Over the course of these forty days, they didn't see an apartment, the ruins of a house or indication of human existence. The good news is that they were informed of this devastation and carried food items that they split into daily meals.

They had enough food to get them through. Then they felt lucky to not be engulfed by an impending snowstorm. Because as they traveled, they came across the remains of travelers who died on their route.

In the end, the Polos made it to the eastern part of the strange region that starts in Balashan and is located just to the north of India. They eventually reached Kashgar, the capital city. Kashgar.

They were now situated on the ground of Cathay and was under the direct supervision by Kublai Khan. Then they were able to pull the talisman of gold and, in honor of the emperor, they could request food, accommodation as well as horses for their lengthy journey.

Finally, Marco was finally in the realm of the legendary Khan. Cathay was older. Cathay was wonderful. Cathay was awe-inspiring and fascinating.

Chapter 5: "Salamander" Cloth

ASHGAR was the most western city in Cathay. Then, after the Polos were able to rest in ASHGAR for a few days, they set off to travel eastward. The country they passed traversed by them was filled with people and abundant in farms. The inhabitants of the area tended to vineyards and gardens and also flax, hemp, cotton and grains. They also traveled through many mountain streams where they discovered the precious jade. The jade they found was across a wide variety and huge quantities.

Marco found three intriguing aspects about the inhabitants in this region one among them was their religious liberty. For those who were from Medieval Europe the concept of religious tolerance was not a common thing. Marco discovered three different forms of worship. Certain worshippers adored Mohammed Some were devoted to Buddha and others which, as Marco was surprised were worshippers of Christ. The two religions, Marco discovered to be in harmony peacefully. Freedom of religious worship, which is a tradition in Cathay was backed by the grand Khan. The Khan let religions be practiced freely.

Who was it that were the Christians whom Marco came across in Far Cathay? Marco asked about them and was able to determine that they were Nestorian Christians. They were disciples of an abbot named Nestorius who, was a young man, around 4000 years after the death of Christ, broke off from his fellow members of the Church of Rome. His doctrines and beliefs differed little from the doctrines of Rome. In consequence, he was demonized and exiled from the church he was a part of. He had a lot of loyal supporters and wherever they went, they carried his ideas and built church. The fifth century was the time when certain of them moved to Cathay in the fifth century, where they were able to enjoy complete religious liberty. They were here for a long time and when Marco Polo arrived their church had been established on Oriental soil.

Another point of interest that Marco observed in the western region of Cathay was the fact that a lot of those present had massive bumps around their necks. He also noted that they are "occasioned by the quality of the water." In the present, medical research has proven the notion that pure mountain water that is not from sea water and thus deficient in iodine is responsible for this swelling that is commonly referred to as goiter. The condition is common, and is still prevalent across western China.

The final thing Marco noticed was an odd rule. In a region called Pein there was a 20-

day statute. When a person departed from his residence and was absent for a period of twenty days or longer, then his wife was entitled to, if inclined, to get a new husband. The new man immediately took over her house!

In the middle of 28 days of travel through the an agriculturally fertile region and lush countryside, the Polos reached town of Lop located at the edge of an extremely dry region that was known as"the Desert of Lop. Camels were utilized as the purpose of a beast of burden as they could ride in the desert more effectively than horses and asses.

When they transferred their luggage onto camels and secure--with the aid of the golden tablet--plans for a complete thirty days traveling, Marco Polo and his uncle and father joined an expedition. The caravan's masters pledged to guard them in the desert. They had a good understanding of the desert and promised to control the trip so that the caravan could be taken to rest every night by fresh water.

Before setting off on the desert, and still living in Lop, the capital city Lop Polo, the Polos received a variety of strange tales of horrors, fears and ghosts.

"There are evil spirits in the desert," warned certain people from Lop. "These spirits lure travellers from their route and bring them to destruction."

"Do not stray from your caravan," advised other travelers, "for it is then when the spirits will do their devilish job. They'll shout your names like they were your family members asking you to listen, but when you listen to them, you'll get sucked into the wrong direction, and eventually lost."

Some others mentioned how an individual traveler could hear the noise of a massive caravan. In the morning, he would continue the same direction in hopes to get on the same side as the group. This would lead him deep into the desert in which he wandered and die.

The Polos were not convinced of those tales of supernatural evil. When their caravan was wandering in the desert, they could hear odd noises in the midnight. The noises, Marco recorded, reminded him of an array of instruments that were all at the same time. Sometimes, in addition to the sounds produced by these instruments, was the sound of drums. The sounds that echoed into the stillness of the desert night, were alarming.

We know today that the noises the Polos experienced and which scared Lop's inhabitants are result of the sands being hot and that cool quickly after sunset. The settling and contraction of vast areas of sand can produce odd sounds, which are similar to music instruments.

Few travelers, up still to this day, traversed the bone-horse covered, desolate desert landscape of Lop. In addition, Marco along with his uncle and father, felt content once the crossing ended and they walked again into a friendly village.

Also in the western region of Cathay where Marco noticed a tradition which he found to be odd. The first thing to note is that the people didn't burial their deceased, rather they the cremated their dead. In addition, when someone passed away the family members did not conduct funeral services. The family members first gathered their temple priests, as well as local Astrologers. Astrologers created the horoscope which revealed how the heavens were positioned by the constellations as well as the stars in the year of birth date of the person who had passed away. Based on this chart, they calculated the most fortunate days and months and then chose one date they believed to be the best to the deceased in making his way to heaven. Therefore, they may decide to delay the funeral by weeks, or in certain cases, up to six months.

To ensure the preservation of an individual's body for this long an amount of time it was common to create a coffin out of solid planks that were several inches wide. The joints were sealed using the mixture of tar with lime. On top of the body was an assortment of gums that smelled sweet as well as camphor, among other substances. When all was securely closed, the unfinished coffin board was covered in colored silk. After that, a table was set up in front of the coffin. There was wines, bread and other dishes of food. The food served was intended meant to please the spirits of the dead who must sit patiently for the perfect day to leave the earth to enter the heavens.

Finally, as the day of long-awaited celebration arrived family and acquaintances gathered to form an eulogy procession. The coffin was carried across the country, to the location for the funeral. The procession sat under the canopies of silk which were put in the roadway. In these places of rest, loved ones and relatives burned an assortment of money from cardboard and paper models of males and females, horses and the other items they wanted their deceased loved ones to own. The spirit of the paper pictures they believed would go to heaven and bring peace for the soul who died. Therefore, he'd have cash when he reached heaven. He would also be able to have horses, servants and other friends.

At the beginning, Marco was of the opinion that this bizarre burial practice was just some local ritual. However, he later discovered that this custom was widespread to everyone in Cathay. This practice has been practiced since the beginning of time and the practice that Marco Polo saw is still practiced by Cathay even to this today.

In the west of Cathay, Marco witnessed the weaving of a cloth that was referred to as salamander cloth. This was a form of fabric made with mineral fibres, which looked like an coarse wool. It was a fossil that was found in the mountains. Marco Polo describes the process according to this: "This, after being exposed to sunlight to dry is crushed in the mortar of brass, after which it is washed until all earthly elements have been removed. The fiber is then cleansed and separated from one another and then turns into threads and are then woven into a cloth." In order to bleach the fabric, it was put in a flame, and the result was as clear as snow.

There was a belief, during Marco Polo's time that the salamander was able to resist fire. It is as a result, Marco named this fabric salamander wool. Today, we recognize this wool mineral under the term asbestos.

One of the odd animals that Marco Polo found in this region The most notable was the Musk Deer, and the second was a Yak. Marco observed that the musk was small in size, comparable to gazelle and was covered in rough hair. Marco was the first person to talk about the bizarre animal that lives in the form of a smelt. He noted that it was no horns, but two tusks in the upper part of its jaw. Musks were kept inside a small sac underneath the hide and in the stomach and on the back of the animal. The animal that was killed the precious sac was removed and dried out in the sunshine. It was incredibly pungent in scent and was later used for Cathay as the base of perfume. In the present, a century after, the most popular French fragrances contain at least in a small amount of this smell that is derived from the specific deer species located in Tibet and Western China.

The Yak, Marco said, was massive, and sometimes up to 6 feet tall. It was very similar to the ugly bull, however the legs of the yak were smaller and were covered with soft and long hair. Like a bull, the yak can be unattractive and even dangerous. Marco was able to see many wild, and a good number who had been trained and turned into animals of heavy burden. The animals were robust; they were able to carry huge loads of weight on their backs, and pulled the cart with ease as a big workhorse.

Apart from these two bizarre creatures, Marco found in this area of Cathay the pure white camel. The hair of the camel was weaved into a exquisite cloth by the indigenous people and was sold to merchants who shipped it across the areas in the Orient. The exquisite cloth was highly sought-after.

Also, here, Marco saw great flocks of a particular type of bird called a pheasant. The bird was stunning and the tail feathers of its are usually six feet long. On stage, the main characters of Chinese stage drama often, even to today, wear huge plumes in their caps.

These were all things Marco observed and documented. They were completely new to him. They were unusual, they were distinct.

As the Polos were getting closer to the vast east cities like Cathay and the palace of the Emperor Kublai Khan, Marco noticed that roads were getting more efficient. Later, he learned that Khan believed that the safety and prosperity of his country depended heavily on a well-maintained and extensive roads system.

With good roads, traders could deliver their goods to various areas of the earth. Also, on these same roads soldiers could easily be transferred from one area into another during moments of need. Also, he believed that having a highway system aid in bringing people together of his country.

The result was that he the construction of a network of roads all over Cathay. These roads, manned by soldiers for the security of travelers, linked to all cities and provinces in the country. Numerous gangs of workers worked continuously to keep the roads in good condition. To ensure the safety of the travelers, Khan had planted trees on all major roads. The trees provided shade during the summer months and slowed the snow during winter. In arid areas where trees were unable to be able to grow, Khan commanded that the stone columns be constructed in order to identify the route to the area that was covered in snow.

Marco wrote that he and his father and uncle stumbled across numerous inns along the route that offered the best comfort. They also resided at state post houses, and secured -with the help of their golden symbol of protection--fresh horses as well as all the other things needed.

The posthouses were operated by the federal government to the convenience and benefit of all travelers, both travelers on own behalf and those working to work for the federal government. The posthouses were equipped with sleeping areas along with all other necessities to the travelers. Travelers on Khan's work were taken care of at no charge.

Stables were attached to every posthouse. Here, fresh horses were exchanged to tired horses. The stables could hold up to thousands of horses to ensure that the speedy postriders of Khan could travel without any delay. Governors, ambassadors, and official of the country were able to traverse long distances in fastest time possible.

The Polos traveled on.

Alongside in addition to the Persian as well as Mongolian languages, which Marco Polo already knew, and with which he developed proficiency on the other side of west Cathay that is located directly to the north of India and China, Marco Polo discovered two other languages. They were Chinese and also the language of the Hindus also known as Hindustani.

Marco was immediately able his sights on learning these languages of the world.

Every chance he had, he spoke with the locals and he was taught to write their unique scripts. There were many pages of instructions that he could try.

In Cathay the population was comparatively small that were familiar with the four principal languages spoken across the Orient. The four languages - Persian, Mongolian, Chinese and Hindustani were spoken by a large number of people throughout the East. The Khan was also the emperor supreme over the vast territory of these four languages. Communication was a key element of his reign. Language, as he understood that was the primary element of the process of communication.

As we'll soon learn is to help make Marco Polo very important in the views of Kublai Kublai Khan. Khan.

THE STORY OF GENGHIS KHAN

THE POLOS TRANSPORTED in and out every day in the direction of the east towards the court Kublai Khan. Then one day, they reached China's Great Wall of China. It was an experience like none Marco has ever witnessed.

The travelers sat on the top of an uphill. In front of them beyond what they could tell the vast serpentine of bricks. It stretched west and eastward all the way to the edge of the horizon. It twisted it's way through mountains, through valleys, and across wide plains.

As the Polos reached an entrance within the Great Wall they stopped to relax and Marco talked to the gatekeeper.

"How long is this wall?" the man inquired.

"It is long," declared the gatekeeper. "Very long. It extends from the ocean to the extreme west which is about 180 miles. The castle was constructed years ago, many centuries years ago.

"How many centuries?" Marco asked. Marco.

"Almost more than enough to be counted. It's about 15 hundreds of years old."

The wall was very old I was the thought of Marco. In the early days before Christ this wall was constructed. It was built about two hundred years prior to Christ's time.

Marco was able to assess the wall. He looked at the masonry blocks and after that, he and the gatekeeper took a staircase towards the highest point. The wall was around twenty-two feet tall and twenty feet in width. From the crest of the wall, he was able to see towers with lookouts that were spaced a hundred yards from each other. The towers stood forty feet high. They were also forty feet tall. that in these and other places across the huge section of wall were gates with arched archways, which were secured with doors of heavy oaken construction.

After that, Marco was curious about why the wall was constructed and who was the person responsible for it.

"Ah!" said the gatekeeper. "It was constructed by the citizens from Cathay and with a compelling motive. The castle was constructed to keep from the brutal Mongolians who were residing in the North. These tribal warriors of Mongolia continuously ravaged peaceful land of Cathay. The wall was constructed in order to protect against the enemies. It was able to do this for a long time, for as long as Mongolian tribes weren't joined. However, one day one of the leaders, Genghis Khan, the grandfather of Khan-Kublai's current Khan-Kublai - united the dispersed tribes, and together with these Mongolian hoards, swept through the gates of the wall, and defeated Cathay."

Marco was intrigued to find out more about the gatekeeper's activities and was able to continue.

"Ah that was so simple actually. It took place in the midnight. A grumpy gatekeeper was paid and the gates were then opened for the enemies. Just one prank as well as the labor and sweat over centuries were deemed worthless."

This was all very interesting and fascinating, as Marco discovered that this was exactly the identical Genghis Khan, and the Mongolian hoards that swept across Asia and created terror across

Europe. They were the exact people that in Europe are known as Tartars.

The gatekeeper was asked to explain the situation.

And as they stood admiring the magnificent Wall of China, the gatekeeper explained to Marco all he could know concerning Genghis Khan, the most powerful conqueror of the past since Alexander. According to the gatekeeper's report, Marco also added a few things was known about the Tartars of Europe.

"It is a cruel history written in blood," told the gatekeeper. "It is the story of the great rise of a simple shepherd boy from the plains of Mongolia." He then shared with Marco the tale of Genghis.

Genghis was the child of a chieftain's petty in the Plains of Mongolia, Genghis had his early years riding in the saddle and chasing animals and horses. The people he fought were nomadic. They traveled with their animals. When the grass was green and they could stay. The tent they slept in was their home.

However, the tents of the Mongols were distinct. First the tents were erected on a wooden base that was equipped with wheels similar to a cart which meant it could be drawn by oxen and controlled the yaks. Tents were made from dense felt, and were supported by wood strips that were woven into baskets. There was an opening that allowed to let air flow. The felt was treated with butter fat that rendered it waterproof. large cords held the tent in place against wind.

A few of the tents placed on large platforms for moving are so big that they needed a number of beasts to move them. The entire family lived in one tent.

The summer months saw people were dressed in woolen fabric that was woven at home and spun. In winter, they would wear the furs of the animals. Women and men had been conditioned. They were great hunters and experienced horsemen. They ridden long-stirrup horses in close to a standing posture. They were able to sit in the saddle for an all day, with no fatigue. The best horsemen in the world could match their performance.

It happened when Genghis was just 13 years old, his father's death came abruptly. The chiefs of adjacent tribes set out to claim the title of master over this tribe, which was without a chieftain.

"We will protect you," declared one.

"Come, join us and we will all be one family," Others exclaimed.

However, the mother of a widowed child told the children: "My son Genghis will take over the kingdom. Genghis will be the chief for the entire tribe."

"He has a young age. People need leaders. They'll rise up against your leadership."

"In his father's place, Genghis will rule," said his mother.

"The most saline wells may be dry and the most hard stone may be cracked. What is the reason your followers should stick to you when they don't have an authority figure? Also is the possibility that some may take aim at your leadership."

However, the young Genghis didn't wait around for his enemies to strike. He immediately set off to prepare and arm younger members from his tribe. In the end, he chose the least strong of the tribes around him, he came into it, without prior warning. His assault was quick fast and brutal. He won.

So he sacked each tribe until he had united several Mongolian tribes.

He persuaded the people were defeated to join his troops and take on others. In the end, all of Mongolia was under his control with the exception of one region which was overseen by an older chieftain. Genghis came to his request and demanded the consent of his daughter to marry.

"After all, are we not all Mongols?" He stated. "Why do we need to fight against us? It is better to be one because then we'd be strong enough and ready to be able to fight against any opponent."

The moment he tied the knot, his daughter, the chieftain's daughter Genghis was regarded as the ruler over Mongolia in general. Mongolia. Then he looked at China's Great Wall of China. Cathay was wealthy. The men he commanded were battle skilled; they were veterans of numerous battles; they were able to devise special military maneuvers and innovative strategies. They were fast. They were brutal. They were brutal. He realized he was prepared to take on the wonderful Cathay.

Then, secretly Genghis Khan was assembling his soldiers on a private portion within the Great Wall. After getting bribed by the gatekeepers, he took his entire army, riding on top horses, past an open gate in the late at night. The next morning, the army began the war of terror. Every village was burned to the ground and the people who refused to leave were shot and murdered.

Genghis believed in lightning-swift strikes. Genghis believed in the power of surprise strikes. He believed in destroying his enemies through sheer force and awe.

The Emperor of China and his family fled Peking and took refuge in the southern region of Cathay. People of Cathay weren't prepared to face the ruthless adversaries. It wasn't long until Genghis the young man, an infant and was crowned the to be the ruler of Cathay and Mongolia.

Feeling elated and enjoying the celebration, Genghis moved his armies towards the west. Never before had an army spanned such an area. There has never been an army that had been as well-trained and well-organized. In most marches, when it was forced in advance, soldiers were each armed with eight horses. Riders would change horses each hour. They could thus travel all day long and at night with no rest. Some of them sat in their saddles but they continued to ride on. If they felt hungry, they would stop for a few seconds, and then break an incision on the horse's leg, and after drinking blood, tie around the horse's injury before continuing to ride.

Genghis split his army into 3 armies. Generals who would lead his right-hand army, Genghis named his brothers. The sons of Genghis led the left armies while Genghis, himself together with his son's youngest, commanded his central armies. Three armies, while totally independent from one another but were united under the single command of his. They allied themselves whenever they needed to.

Genghis conceived of new military maneuvers and tactics. Genghis believed in long, extensive preparations, surprising attacks, and the strength of the fear of. Sometimes, he would use his army centrally for attacking. When the adversary would be able to take on the force, two side armies would emerge and, as if nutscrackers, rip the life of the enemy.

Another strategy used by Genghis was to send an unimportant force forward in the midst of his main army back. This tiny force, with the intention of confronting an enemies, would claim that they were in a desperate battle and then retreat. The adversaries, convinced that they would be able to overwhelm this smaller forces, would then pursue their retreat and then be lured into a carefully-planned trap. Soon, they were completely isolated and hopelessly defeated.

Utilizing this strategy, with these tactics, the Mongolian forces of Genghis were able to march triumphantly from one side of Asia towards the opposite. The barbaric cruelty of Genghis struck fear to the hearts of every one. The lands they conquered were incorporated into Genghis Khan's empire.

In the end, after most of Asia was his, and when his army swarmed to the border to

Greater Turkey, Genghis decided that he was now in control of sufficient territories. Genghis sent a message of peace to the shahs of Turkey.

"I have no need of other lands," the message said in the message. "I take it that we have an equal interest in encouraging trade between our subjects."

The shah was reportedly agreeable. The first trader that was carried across the borders by Genghis was taken over from the city's governor by one of Turkish cities. The participants of the group were sentenced to death for spies.

Genghis immediately demanded his satisfaction. Genghis demanded the head of the governor. However, the shah became overly confident, and not just would he not surrender to the governor, but also took off the heads of Tartar representatives, who Genghis had sent to

Genghis with his request. The heads were gave to Genghis with the highest praises.

This is how wars usually start. Diplomacy is ineffective because pride stops the mistakes of others from being acknowledged. Inattention can lead to arrogance. arrogance can lead to insults. A snide comment can lead to war.

Genghis declared that he would get his revenge. His revenge was to launch an offensive that would be one of the most shocking ever seen in the history of the world. This war not only altered the landscape of some areas of the globe, but also it also brought Mongolians and Turks to Europe. Every Western civilizations began to shake.

Genghis didn't launch his battle against the shah without meticulous pre-planning. He was a bit irritated by the insult, but he did not act with a shrewd deliberation. He waited until spring of the year, before he took one of his army to Turkey. The shah led an army that was four hundred thousand soldiers however, in the fights following they were destroyed, with nearly one third of them being killed. The shah fled in the hope of saving what was left from his troops and was subsequently faced with a new Mongolian army that arrived at random before him. He had no idea what he was in for on. But another Mongolian army entered Turkey in order to burn villages and towns and to kill everyone, including women, men and even children.

In the end, the shah ran away terrified. There was no safe place. There was no place he could stay indefinitely. In one instance, he was compelled to hide himself as a poor priest and to seek refuge in mosques.

Each time, the rich and proud walled cities of his country were taken over. The siege could last for about six or seven months prior to the city, stricken with desperation, was made to give up its territory. A long-running siege ravaged Bokhara. Bokhara. Once the Mongols arrived, Genghis was at the top of his army. Genghis drove his horse up the steps leading to the main mosque and then on the terrace he yelled to his troops: "The hay is cut; give your horses fodder." It was his means of saying that his job was finished and his troops were free to take out and pillage. The city was a proud one and no one escaped alive. The city was stripped all valuable items, and then was smashed to pieces. However, the shah continued to be hunted. After a while the shah was diminished to a beggar and alone the shah on his flight, reached the shores of Caspian Sea. There, because of long suffering and adversity the shah died.

However, the news of shah's demise didn't reach Genghis his army, who continued in their pursuit, wrecking everything in their way. A vast majority of Turkish citizens, terrified of a advancing enemy left the west to Europe. This is how powerful inflicting insults.

The Mongolian army now crossed over across the Caucasian Mountains into Russia. They laid broad roads across the forests, over the mountains, where they drove carts in tented cabs. Then they reached the enormous Russian plains that offered excellent pastures for their cattle and horses.

The majestic Russian city of Kiev as well as Moscow were under siege for a number of months, and after they were destroyed to the slaughter, all of them were killed, with only one exception: youngsters who were held in captivity and sold as slaves.

However, anger remained inside Genghis and the army marched towards him. The King of Poland hesitated. In a desperate attempt, he pleaded for help against the invading barbarians. He wrote to Pope Francis in which he stated that Christianity was in danger of extinct. The Pope did not send any aid. Poland was destroyed and the king fled.

In the meantime, the cities of Hungary was destroyed. As the time approached for winter, the troops of Genghis established their camp along the eastern banks of the Danube River. They waited there for the spring to arrive.

Europe was in a weak state. Europe was weak. Dark Ages were still over and the populace. The centuries of ignorance had crippled their minds. The centuries of mythology and bizarre religions had wrecked their belief in reality and their ability to resist invasion. The Moors were already in Spain and had met with only a little resistance. How could they stop the Tartars from their victory Westward marches?

As strange as it might appear, once spring came around the Tartars were not advancing over the Danube. Actually, they started to pull their troops back to Asia. It was an enormous comfort for Europe. However, the motive behind this retreat Europeans didn't know.

But, there was an important motive. This is the reason Marco Polo now learned-- among the various other aspects was learned from this incredible conqueror Genghis. Genghis's Mongolian army did not carry on their assault on Europe in the winter of 1818, because was a time of illness Genghis, the legendary Genghis unexpectedly died.

His death was kept private. The body of the deceased was transported by a grand funeral procession across Asia towards his native country of Mongolia. To stop the information about his demise from spreading to the public, everyone along the route who were able to witness the funeral procession was taken into custody and shot dead. According to the records, during this parade, 20 thousand innocent people were killed.

Genghis was laid to rest in a grave hidden from view, with every ritual of the traditional religious practices of Genghis was buried in a secret grave with all the primitive religious rites of Mongolians. To this day, the precise site of his burial is not known.

The child of a chieftain from the nomads, Genghis had lived to construct the best military equipment to be seen by the entire world. He was alive to see his army of victorious soldiers spread across all of Asia and across a significant portion of Europe. He was able to rule over more territories than any emperor throughout all the history of mankind. He set up principles for war that were fresh and uncompromising. He declared war upon entire people, and on the enemy armed.

In the year Genghis passed away in the year 1227, his son Kublai was just thirteen years old. of age. However, he was already fighting alongside his grandfather who defeated him. At a young age, he began to master the techniques of Mongolian combat.

In the year 1947, just forty-seven months after the death of his father, Kublai was on the supreme throne of the vast kingdom. In the meantime, he waited eagerly to hear the news of the Italian merchants he given to the Pope to serve as his envoys. He waited patiently for those a hundred people educated who would be invited to the court of his. He was well aware of the fact that it was an extremely long trip between Cathay through Rome and then back. Yet, so many years had gone by between the time that the Polo merchants had gone and the Khan almost gave the hope of seeing the merchants once more.

However, one day his couriers informed him of the Polo merchants, along with the child of one of the brothers, had been discovered along the route to the court of his. But they were far away from the court, which will require another forty days.

In the wake of this, the Khan was pleased. The Khan sent officers out with fresh horses to welcome those who had travelled for a long time and ensure that they were provided with everything they could need for their well-being. He also instructed the officers to take the Polos to his palace at minimum delay.

They did. With royal escort, the Polos were now able to ride forward towards the capital city of Cathay.

The ruins of the old Peking that was destroyed by the infamous Genghis, Kublai Khan, his grandson, had constructed the city of his dreams. The city that was the capital of his empire was given the name Cambalu the word is in Mongolian signifies "City of the Khan".

This is where, in an impressive marble palace, which was surrounded by lavish luxury and immense riches gathered from faraway regions, Kublai Khan waited patiently to see the arrival of the Polos.

Chapter 6: "Where Are The Hundred Men Of Learning?"

IN THE LARGE auditorium of the palace, three Polos kneeled on the floor before the Khan. They bow their heads at the carpet 4 times. However, the Khan promptly ordered them to get up and greeted them with a warm welcome.

He was happy to have his ambassadors at court. They kept their promises that they would return to him regardless of travel that had been wrought with risks and lots of hardships.

When the Khan was done with his greetings, Nicolo presented his son.

"May this please you Majesty that I present to you my nephew Marco. Marco will be here for to serve you."

Marco acknowledged him with a respectful bow.

The Khan smiled. There was something in Marco's radiant facial features that he appreciated. Also, the Khan could not resist recognizing the sparkling intelligence that was his eyes.

He was able to ask Marco numerous questions, and was amazed to discover the ease with which he could speak Mongolian. When Kublai discovered that young Marco was also fluent in Persian, Hindustani and Chinese He was extremely impressed. Kublai said that after the next day or so in the future, once they had a good rest He wanted to visit them once more. He was particularly interested in speaking with Marco and to hear about their adventures during their lengthy journey. Khan told him that he wanted to find out more about the thousands of individuals in his huge kingdom. They were his subjects. They were his subjects. He wanted to find out everything about their lives.

When the Khan spoke, Marco noticed that he was extremely weighty. He was still of medium size, meaning that his height was neither excessively high or too small. The body of his was in the right proportions and his skin seemed to be. The eyes of his were dark and attractive, while his nose was very large, but nicely shaped. This Marco observed as he stood on the shoulders of Khan.

The Khan continued to speak. He looked at the elder Polos and he asked him: "Where are the hundred men of learning which I desired?"

Then Marco's uncle and father stepped into the room to clarify the events that had transpired. They informed the Khan all the details. They explained to him why they'd been delayed for so long and also how they were able to see the pope of their dreams. They also told of the two friars who were terrified. They also said they were carrying present and letters which they received from the Pope was sending.

The gifts were taken into the palace's hall, where they were wrapped. The presents were then placed on steps that led to the King's throne. They were then translated and was read. However, the Khan did not feel satisfied. He was dissatisfied with the correspondence and was not satisfied with the gifts. It was an inadequate alternative to the 100 students he wanted to get from Europe. The Khan believed that the beauty of a country is not based on silver or gold, however, rather it's in learning. He believed that learning is the key to understanding, and leads to enlightenment.

Then he raised his hand, and he was able to have the present from the Pope taken away from his view. He was sad, yet was not blaming the Polos in the debacle of their task. He stated this clearly and, in more than a hundred different ways, he showed his guests that they are welcome. The robes were even presented to them. of honor, which he gave to the guests. He even made the ladies wear these impressive gowns before his eyes.

"And now that you are safely returned to my court, here you will remain," he declared. "And never again will I send you on so long and so perilous a journey."

The Khan was able to see that they were tired of their journeys and didn't want to delay his conversation in their presence. He ordered them to have their own rooms at the palace. He also instructed that royal chefs would prepare their meals according to what they preferred the best. He also urged the Polos to relax and added that he was looking forward to seeing them very shortly.

PAPER MONEY

VERYTHING WAS NEW. It was all new. What was the way to get Marco to relax with plenty to do?

After leaving his parents and uncle left behind, he walked immediately into the stunning city of Cambalu which was adorned with tiled roofs as well as its towers of stone as well as its wide, roads that were paved. Cambalu was the capital city of the huge Empire of the Khan. He walked the streets for hours after hours. Many streets and roads! There were artisans working on their products in shops that were open. He sat down with people. There was a lot to explore as well as a lot to be learned.

Marco quickly discovered his city Cambalu was actually two cities that were separated by a tiny river. The north side of the river was the actual city of Cambalu that Kublai Khan had constructed on the ruin of Peking. The Khan was however the day astrologers informed him that the city was planning to rebel against him. So he made a decision to build a brand new city on the southern side of the river. The city was named Taidu. After it was complete, the Khan shifted all residents of the city to the new city. Only those who had loyalties he believed in to stay in the old Cambalu. Since the amount of his loyal subjects was to be quite substantial Both cities were populous.

Marco discovered the two cities were surrounded by walls. The wall in the old city was built from brick, whereas the wall in the new city, that formed the perfect square composed of pounded soil. The base's width was around ten feet and the height on top was three yards. All the battlements were painted white. The wall also contained twelve gates. When constructing this city, the Khan had directed that the streets be constructed in squares and with plenty of room given to parks and gardens.

Within the middle of this modern city Marco discovered a magnificent bell hanging from an edifice. While he was looking at it, he questioned an elderly man who was passing by, what is the significance of this bell might be.

"Ah," said the old man "this bell serves a beneficial reason. Every night, it announces an order to shut down. Once it has the tones of warning that night, nobody is permitted to go out except for those who are on business."

"Do all obey this curfew?" Marco asked. Marco.

"Of course," said the elderly man. "Special guards patrol the streets at night to see that this regulation is obeyed!"

While walking through the streets in each city, it was weird and alien to Marco. How people behave, the customs and food habits, the dress code street, houses and the crowds that throbbed as well as their sounds... In front of his eyes was a world that was old; But for him, this was a new place. It was a country that was as old as it gets one, and a place that was rich in history. This was a culture that has never been witnessed before as fully documented by an explorer from Europe.

Marco took a break for a while in the colorful bazaars of Cambalu. Every every day, came caravans filled with wealth. They came from various regions of the

Empire. There were a variety of stands and shops, sheltered by bright awnings, it was possible to purchase woollens, silks, jewellery made from jade, crystal and gold and also expensive decorations, hangings and brocades, carpets and even places. There were other stores that selling vegetables, fruits as well as meats and food items as well as various kinds of spices. There were areas where the sale of drugs and plants were available in addition to other areas where household items and kitchenware were sold. There were also booths where made of brass and copper nearby were places that had tailors and shoemakers working. Nearly everything one wanted was available in the thriving bazaars in Cambalu and even slave women with fair skin and amazing beauty.

But The Khan, Marco learnt, was adamant about people who wanted to make a huge gain. The Khan had a group comprised of appraisers for commercial purposes to review every item and determine the rates at which they would be sold to ensure an acceptable gain. The traders were in agreement with this since once the general public was aware that they were getting a fair price and they could buy with no any hesitation. Therefore, goods were immediately taken away.

All things were sold to make money. Even the currency from Cathay was a bit strange for Marco. There were tiny brass coins that had round holes at the center. These were known as "cash" and were strung with long strings. Also, there were squares of silver, as well as bars as many items were valued in ounces silver. The merchants even used scales in their shops for weighing the silver. Additionally, there were some silver coins available. Back home, Marco was accustomed to coinage made of gold and silver. In Cathay He discovered a brand new type of money: paper!

Marco was astonished by one merchant about the currency. "I am not sure the reason why you would accept this currency in the same way as gold or silver. It is clear that paper isn't as useful. The thing is that in Europe the continent I'm from, there is only the metal coins that are used in trade, which include copper as well as silver and gold."

The shopkeepers smiled. He was able to see that the foreigner from some faraway land was a bit confused, and was trying to clarify Marco Marco the entire information he had about this currency on paper.

"It is very simple," He explained. "These notepapers are made out of wood and are given by Kahn's government. Every note is secured in the treasury with bullion. Each note's value is clearly outlined, like you see and you are able to swap this note at the treasury to purchase gold. When it gets damaged and old the note can be traded for new paper money with the paying a fee of just a few dollars."

"But how do people know that this paper money is genuine?"

"Ah," said the merchant. "Counterfeiting is a serious crime and punishable by death."

Marco took time to study a variety of paper notes carefully. The front of each note was a illustration of dragons as well as the amount of money the note was worth. Every note was stamped with the vermilion seal.

"That is the vermilion seal of Kublai Khan," stated the seller, pointing. "His seal guarantees the value of this currency."

Marco was attentive and listened to the words written in vermilion. "The Seal of Him who upholds the Kingdom and rules the Nations."

"Yes," continued the merchant, "without the Khan's seal this currency would be worthless, but with it this paper money is freely accepted all over Cathay."

The concept of paper money was not widely known throughout Europe back then And, some years later, after Marco returned to his home after Cathay the people of Cathay would not accept his claim of the value of this money. Nobody could imagine that paper would be able into a currency that could be comparable to silver or gold.

A different and intriguing thing Marco noticed when he walked around the city was a clock made of water. It was a timer in the following manner: A small bathtub of water placed on top of a tub the bamboo spigot inside the top tub, water fell slow, dropping a drop at one moment. Inside the bottom tub was marked by lines and, by observing how much water was in the tub one could see the hour in the morning. The enigmatic method of measuring time was a success. Marco was able to find these clocks atop numerous bridges as well as various other public spaces within the city. These were put there to facilitate ease of use for people.

After lunch, and before returning at the palace Marco went up the steps of some of the gates to city, and was seated on the high above the wall of the city. In front of him, which stretched over several miles to the countryside, he could see the sprawling suburbs of the city of great size. In these areas lived thousands of people that could not locate a home inside the city's walls. There were a number of hotels in which visitors and merchants who traveled.

To the other side in the opposite direction, inside the city walls in Taidu, Marco could see out to the left the palace of the legendary Khan Kublai, mounted like the crown jewel of its gorgeous gardens and beautiful gardens of green.

Chapter 7: In The Palace Of Kublai Khan In Cambalu

The next day, Marco was called into Khan's office. The Khan was amazed by the first encounter with Marco, that he wanted to speak with him in private. He was interested in hearing about the places far away that the Polos traveled. He was fascinated by the way of life and manners they used to live. He was curious about what they did and how they lived as well as what they ate, and the way they entertained themselves. He wanted to find out whether they were poor or wealthy. He was fascinated by gemstones, minerals and various products produced across the different regions. He had a hundred questions were on his mind. Then Marco could answer to Khan's delight.

At times, Marco used to consult his notes. He was then able to tell the Khan specific names for locations they went through, as well as other precise specifics.

When they first met, it was a quick and efficient time for both Marco as well as the Khan. They shared so many things and shared interests that they truly loved each other's company. The meeting also marked the beginning of their long relationship.

The morning they parted, before they left that morning, the Khan gave a tour guide to Marco. This guide's job was to accompany Marco for a walk around the palace as well as its gardens. However, the grandeur of the structure of the palace, as well as the grounds that it was in and the surrounding park, that it couldn't be all seen in one day. After several hours that Marco could finally see the entire thing. The grand palace constructed from marble was spread over vast areas. The building was just one story tall, however it was equivalent to two floors, which is how tall were its ceilings. The palace was bordered from all sides by large terraces running along the edges that had stone balustrades that were adorned with pilasters. The terraces beyond these were parks and gardens of the palace.

The palace's interior was made up of numerous apartments as well as large halls. Apart from the audience chamber where the throne of Khan was set on a dais, there were different chambers that were used by his state ministers in the administration of his empire. Additionally, there were several venues for events and banquets.

Within one of the wings was an enormous apartment that was used by Khan himself. Khan himself. There was a separate wing with areas where tapestries and rugs were made, rooms that were used by royal artists as well as areas for the creation of costumes and embroidery. In this wing, there was a hall in which one hundred scholars would be busy every day translating classics from Cathay into Mongolian dialect. Another wing were rooms reserved for the royal astronomers hired by Khan. In a basement made of stone was a lab where the alchemists from the royal family were working. They worked all day working to create gold using bases metals, as well as making an elixir that would enable people to live 100 years.

There were a lot of rooms and halls, and multiple activities taking place simultaneously it was bustling. Apart from the halls for state, the royal workrooms, and the Khan's personal residence There were additionally adjacent to the huge palace rooms and kitchens that were used by the palace's guards and servants.

Marco was in all of these chambers and halls. He also saw lots of items he'd previously never witnessed. He asked many questions.

When he visited the room for the throne, Marco was able to see the white woolen coat, which was placed in a place next to the throne.

"Whose coat is this?" I asked Marco. "And why does it hang here?"

"This simple woollen coat," stated the source, "once belonged to the Khan's famous grandpa Genghis. Although Genghis defeated the majority of the world, and established the current dynasty the man he was until his last years a humble man of an unassuming taste. He didn't appreciate things of the world. The coat he wore was the only one he wore."

Marco was interested and looked at the coat with great care. The coat was actually a very simple coat. It was made from ordinary natural wool.

The tour guide went on. "This coat is considered revered by the Mongolians. The coat has been hung on the throne, so that when someone is bowing before Khan, He is bowing in the memorial of Genghis The creator of the dynasty."

Marco was unable to resist noticing that stark contrast in the simplicity of the grandpa's jacket and the lavish luxury that surrounded Kublai's grandson. Kublai. He kept his thoughts his thoughts to himself while Marco and his guide left the area.

In the background of the Palace Marco was shown numerous huge structures. These were belongings of the Khan, including his silver and gold bullion and precious stones, pearls as well as vessels of silver and gold.

Just a few yards away from the buildings were a different group of structures that contained apartments for the Khan's wives as well as his concubines. The guide told Marco his wife that Khan was married to four women who were of first rank along with numerous concubines. Each of his wives was a princess or an empress. Also, the son who was born to any of them could be the next heir to the throne.

Concubines of his were ladies with extraordinary beauty. According to the guide, they were selected by following a specific method.

"The Khan has special commissioners who are experts in the appraisal of feminine beauty," the official said. "And it is the duty of these commissioners to journey to all parts of Cathay to select for the Khan's palace the most beautiful girls in the whole land."

It was a fascinating practice for Marco as it was the case that in Europe the custom was not widely practiced. Marco urged his guide to provide more details.

"These commissioners are sometimes able to bring to Cambalu a hundred beautiful girls in a single year," the guide said. the guide. "But typically, they don't have the luxury of bringing so numerous. Their requirements are very quite high. They're very critical even when they are looking at the finest beautiful things they spot some imperfections."

"By what standards is a girl judged fitting to be brought to the court?" was the question posed by Marco.

"Ah, the commissioners have a system of rating beauty in which they give points for special features," said the guide. "A specific amount of points are awarded to the hair, the shape of the lips, beauty of the body's symmetry as well as the eye's grace as well as eyebrow arch as well as other features. The points are taken together, and only girls with a good score will be taken to the palace at Cambalu."

"Do not the parents object to having their daughters taken from them?" was the question asked by Marco.

"Of of course there is no way. Parents consider it to be an honor to be able to keep daughters on the court. They also realize that inside the palace, the daughter is well looked after and might one day marry a prince, minister of state or other officer of high rank."

The instructor then explained as the beautiful young ladies arrived at the palace, they were entrusted with the duties of tuterons and matrons. They were presented with royal dresses as well as instructed on proper dress of court. The ones who had special skills received lessons in dance, music and embroidery, as well as painting or writing.

After the training period finished, the trainees were split into five groups. They were all part of the Khan inside his chambers. Every group occupied his residence for three days. Then an additional group would be in their spot. All through the year, these groups shifted from one to the next.

The author further stated that the Khan could pick one of his stunning ladies and, with her permission, propose her to be a bridesmaid for an unfaithful prince from another country or a faithful minister.

"When one of the Khan's beautiful girls is selected to become a bride," according to an official, "then there is a huge excitement in the palace. The bride's special dress is designed specifically to suit the girl. They shower her with gifts. Also, the Khan will fill her with luxurious furs, silks and crystal, jade, as well as silver-plated ornaments, even decorated ivories as well as rare porcelains. The princesses of every country gets a better inheritance!"

The tour guide then led Marco through the grounds and surrounding parks of the palace. He saw gorgeous trees, rolling meadows, lawns and grasses. The meadows where grazing were gazelles, deer, and a variety of other animals that were peaceful. The visitor saw peacocks as well as many beautiful wild bird species. The streams and lakes of the park were filled with fish. Stone bridges carved with beautiful design spanned the stream. There were also flowers and fruit trees and pagodas for gardens made from lacquered bamboo and trimmed with the beaten silver and gold.

In the middle of the park was a second palace. It was less spacious as the one of Khan, but just as gorgeous. "Here lives the Khan's eldest son Chinkin," told the guide. "He is the heir to the throne. He is the eldest of the Khan's 22 sons with the four women he has married."

Nearby to this second palace was a magnificent mound, known as"the Green Mount. At the center of the mount was an attractive green pagoda, that was surrounded by stunning and unique evergreen trees. Marco was very impressed with its beauty. Green Mount and he stood all day long admiring it.

"The Kahn loves these trees," stated the guide. "Whenever he hears of an unusually rare specimen he orders that it should be carefully dug up, brought to Cambalu and planted here."

The guide also pointed to the buildings along with a huge meadow that was behind The Green Mount. "Those are the Khan's stables," the guide said. "In those tables are stalls for the Khan's thousand white horses."

"A thousand white horses!"

"Yes you can, there are a thousand horses. These white horses are considered sacred. They're well-cared to ensure their health and for breeding horses for the numerous ones needed by the Khan's army." He remained quiet for a few seconds and after that he said: "The mares are milked which is then produced into a clotted Kumiss. Personally, I don't like the flavor of this particular kumiss however it is a favorite of the Khan and his family enjoy this kumiss tremendously. It is considered a delicacy by them."

The guide has now steered Marco to.

The gardens and palace of Khan were surrounded by two massive walls that were set in the another. The wall on the outside divided the property of Khan from the city. The wall inside enclosed the palace of Khan and the garden.

In between the two walls, were the Khan's army and storehouses for military use. Special armouries were built that were specifically designed for the stores. Bridles, saddles stirrups, and other gear from the cavalry occupied the storehouse. Bows, strings quivers, arrows and various objects of archery also occupied a different structure. Armour and breastplates made of a hardened leather took up the third storehouse as well as other items for the branches that required the military's equipment.

The walls of the palace were not controlled by Khan's army, however, the Khan himself as well as his magnificent palace was protected with a specific bodyguard. This bodyguard was comprised of men who were large, with some nearly huge. In addition, Marco was shocked by the fact that these guys were almost all Christians. Marco was interested to learn the origins of these men and the reason why Khan chose them to be his bodyguards.

"These Christians," said the guide, "are descendants of captives who were taken by Genghis. Their grandparents were born in remote regions near those of the Caucasian Mountains."

"Oh, I know where those lands are!" Marco said. Marco. "We travelled near them on our journey from Europe."

"Then you should be aware of the following Christians. A few belong to the Greek church, while others are known as Nestorian believers."

Marco was, naturally, had knowledge of the Greek church that was located in Asia Minor and he had talked to Nestorian's priests from western Cathay.

"But tell me," He said, "why the Khan employs Christians for his bodyguard."

The man spoke with confidence. "You can see that there is a lot of rivalry within the palace among the Mongols as well as Chinese. Chinese as well as the Khan extremely wisely seeks an elite bodyguard that is distinct from the rest, one that isn't easily mingled with other groups. A group like this he believes will not easily be drawn into Palace tensions." He laughed. "Do you know what the Khan calls these Christians?"

"No," said Marco.

"Well the Lord calls them "the luminous ones" because when they speak of God, their faces shine with joy! They're extremely fervent faith-seekers."

All of these were aspects Marco discovered from his earliest days at the palace of Kublai Khan in Cambalu.

A PATRON OF THE ARTS

In the days that followed, Marco and the Khan enjoyed many hours of conversation. They spoke about all sorts of subjects that intrigued their interests. The Khan was interested in knowing what life was like in Europe as well as how it differed from what was happening in Cathay. He was very attracted by the distinctions that Marco explained to him.

He also was curious to know Marco which thing about Cathay that he thought was the most unique. Marco took a moment to think about it and then replied: "Religious freedom".

The Khan was shocked by his response, since he was of the opinion it was obvious that within Europe there must be a lot of tolerance for religion. After Marco has explained his explanation to Khan that this wasn't true and that this was not the case, the Khan declared his opinion regarding this issue.

"It is a tenet of mine to never interfer with the religious beliefs of any sect that is part of my realm. I respect all of them equally. Actually, I defend every religion and do not allow indifference of one group against the other. In fact I think that all people ought to be worshipping whatever god they want to."

Marco was especially fascinated by the words of the Khan. He wanted to know more.

The Khan continued to state that he was himself uncertain about the authority of gods. He claimed that he frequently requested his faithful subjects to prove to him the strength that their gods had. They were gods of the highest quality was those who were able to hear the prayers of their followers and granted them the favors they asked by them. Gods who refused to pay and ignored his wishes were considered to be untrue and not worthy. He claimed to be always skeptical, but eager to believe and above all was his acceptance of the right of others to be convinced.

Khan continued. Khan continued. "Religious freedom was a reality in Cathay prior to the time my famous grandfather won the land. It was in those days that, like you can see today it was populated by Buddhists, Mohammedans, Idolaters, Christians and Jews, who worshipped and lived alongside each other with peace. A lot of them intermarried just like we do today. As of this moment in my court, there are Tartar princes that have married Christians."

Marco was astonished by the words of Khan. Marco didn't know there were Jews within Cathay and he was eager to learn more about them.

"As early as the seventh century," the Khan stated, "large numbers of Jews fleeing from Arabia and Persia in which they were forcibly evicted by the Mohammedans sought shelter in Cathay. In Cathay they've been in peace for decades. They remain peaceful and can worship at their synagogues without restriction. They are referred to as the descendants of Adam who was the first man. Recently, they had a synagogue that burned through fire, I rebuilt it with my own money. In actual fact my doctor of choice who is a man with a wealth of knowledge and culture, is one of the Jew."

The Khan reiterated his belief in freedom of religion. He stated that intolerance is unwholesome, and is caused by ignorance. People who practice intolerance is tend to suffer from that they are being abused by intolerance.

The Khan did not speak for a moment and then smiled in a smile that seemed to be friendly "It matters not," He stated, "what gods my subjects revere. For my birthday, as you can see the entire Cathay ask for well-being and health."

And Marco found out that this was the case.

Khan Kublai's birthday was celebrated on the 22nd date of the month of September. The day before the birthday arrived Ambassadors, rulers, and representatives began to gather in Cambalu. They came from every part of the Orient and brought gifts to the Khan. They included chieftains of distant Mongolian tribes as well as princes from countries who owed their allegiance to. They brought gold bars as well as jewels vase of jade, crystals and other accessories. A few were from The Far North, which is today known as Siberia have brought with them precious sables, rare pelts and Ermine.

However, there were a lot of people as well, who made use of this opportunity to send requests to Khan seeking special favors. Many wanted to be made as city governors, while others were seeking an increase to a higher position or in a titles. Others sought positions as tax collectors, or any other jobs that were lucrative. In fact, there were hundreds of people who came every year with petitions the Khan set up a group consisting of twelve barons, to take such requests and decide those that appeared decent and worth the effort.

In the end, as the day of September 28th came, at all locations of worship under the lands of his rule--such as synagogues, churches as well as temples and mosques -- incense was burned and candles lit. The title of Kublai was honored in the heavens. Every one who was a loyal servant of Kublai paid tribute on this date of Kublai's birth.

On the evening of the day, the celebration of a birthday was held in the banquet hall at the palace of Cambalu. In this hall as well as on this particular occasion, Marco and the elder Polos joined the honoured guests around a table, together with princes from abroad.

Marco was able to observe that at the gathering, the seating arrangements were very odd. The Khan took a seat at a tiny high table that ran to the full length of the space. To his left was one of his wives. To left were his grandchildren, sons and other relatives via blood. This table was less than the table that the Khan was sitting. Nobles and princes also had seating at lower tables. The same went for wives of grandchildren, the sons of the Khan and women from the court. They were all placed at the left flank. Also, there were tables reserved to the wives of ministers as well as military officials. Everyone was seated according to the respective rank and honors.

But, everyone that had gathered to honor the birthday of the Khan couldn't be allowed to be accommodated in the main room. Most of the attendees ate their meals on carpets in the other rooms.

To celebrate this event, the Khan was attired in his most exquisite robes. They were made of threads of pure gold. He was wearing his official jewels along with a gold belt. The guests and relatives of his were dressed in expensive garments made of silk and the belts made of silver and gold. Many of these exquisite costumes were presented for them by Khan himself. The costumes of the people who were those whom the Khan was awed by included real jewelry and pearls. Marco believed that some of these costumes had a amount of ten thousand pounds of gold. In all his years, he has never ever seen such a stunning appearance.

Once everyone had found their homes Stewards and staff members brought in a variety of meals for the guests. A variety of food to consume Marco could not have imagined. The Khan is however served by a few of his barons who had their mouths and noses lined with fine, embroidered handkerchiefs in order to ensure that the wine and food would not be affected from their breath.

When the Khan demanded a drink, and when the drink was given to him, the people who were serving him, as well as the other guests in the hall kneeled on the ground and bow to the floor to him in respect. While they were bowing, the musicians started playing. The music continued to play until the Khan had finished drinking. All the guests was again seated and went back to the banquet. Then, as many times as Khan consumed his drink, the ceremony was repeated!

When the dinner was finished, upon the signal of the Khan the performers like tumblers, jugglers as well as other entertainers were allowed into the room and began to perform their talents. After they had were done, their spots were taken by dancers as well as musicians. Then, Khan summoned his yellow lamas. Dark priests with amazing yellow turbans said that they had the power to control weather by generating sunlight or rain at the touch of a button. They also claimed that they had other supernatural abilities. Actually, all their magic tricks, they stated, were created via the power of the supernatural. In addition, because they desired to convince the Khan to believe they were possessed of these amazing abilities, they refused to reveal to anyone the magic tricks they used were accomplished.

As soon when they entered the hall they walked up to the table of Khan and, in a dramatic manner at the same time, demanded of the Khan to reach out his hands. And, before the eyes of everyone, they caused an opulent golden cup to raise, move in a slow, steady manner before settling with his hands outstretched. Once the Khan had drank from the goblet of gold, they made the wine pitcher to fly unaided across the air, and to pour freshly brewed wine into the Goblet of Khan. After this the pitcher floated returning to its spot in the slumber. The feat they performed for the entertainment of Khan and the guests.

The Yellow Lamas were masters at the art of mystification and illusion. In the later years as Marco traveled across Cathay for the benefit of the Khan and the Khan of Cathay, he would often stay for a night in monasteries owned by the lamas. He was always amazed by the feats they performed. However, he quickly discovered that the Red Lama of Cathay which was a sect that rivaled were viewed by their Yellow fellows with extreme disdain. They branded them as unorthodox and claimed that they were just cheap tricksters and a swindler. However, the Yellow Lamas could perform a variety of amazing magic tricks that even until today, have not been duplicated by any of our world-renowned magicians.

But, it was during the birthday celebration of Khan Marco first witnessed a show presented by the Yellow Lamas. The illusions they crafted during this event were amusing and also enthralling. There were plenty of people with a deep belief that the holy men possessed supernatural abilities.

The Yellow Lamas completed their displays of magic, the dinner ended. They then retreated and went home.

Another celebration that was enjoyed throughout Cathay included The White Feast or New Year's Day. The day of celebration was considered to be the most important celebration of the year, and on this day, the Khan was again presented with gifts and served a feast.

However, for the day Khan and his entourage didn't dress with gold or dazzling silks. Instead, they wore clothes of white because it was believed to symbolize luck. Also, throughout Cathay on this day, the citizens, as per to their beliefs, wore things in white to ensure prosperity in the new year. The day was full of celebration everywhere, and everyone were embracing each other, saying: "May good fortune attend you through the coming year, and may everything you undertake succeed to your wish."

On this day when the Khan presented his elephants, of which he owned a number of thousand through Cambalu's streets. Cambalu. The animals were lavishly adorned with rugs of richness and were adorned with colorful howdahs in which were riding guests of the court. The atmosphere was festive and fun.

Inside the palace, those princes and princesses in the realm as well as nobles of all ranks as well as members of the Khan's family gathered in a large room. As they sat sitting in their seats one noble of high standing stood and spoke with an ebullient voice: "Bow down and do reverence!" All were kneeling and touching their foreheads down. The same thing was repeated four times. After that, the noble walked towards an altar on the table was a red tablet engraved by his name and the initials of the Khan. With burning incense, it was perfumed on the tablet and altar. While he was doing this the entire congregation and reverently lowered their heads.

The ceremony ended and the guests were served a dinner following which was a stage performance performed by members of Khan's Imperial Theatre. After the show was finished, everybody returned to their own residence.

Marco discovered in addition to other details it was discovered that Khan was the very first emperor of Cathay to promote the growth of the theater. Prior to his time the actors were just wandering minstrels. Then it was Khan Kublai who brought together the most talented actors of Cambalu and also gave them cash to create the very first Imperial Theatre of Cathay.

Apart from helping actors, Khan helped the poets and writers of the time and also novelists and playwrights. He was extremely fond of performers, writers and artists. He offered them the things they needed in order to ensure they could spend their entire time on their craft. Numerous works of literature as well as numerous amazing paintings created during the time of Khan remain to this today and remain highly admired. Without the patronage of the Khan, they may never be created.

In spite of the horrific stories of the Mongolians that Marco knew about the Mongolians during his time in Europe He was astonished by the court of the king in the royal court, to discover this high level of civilization. What was the way the grandson of brutal Genghis Khan would be one of the most educated and well-educated? The answer is simple.

Although the Mongolians were primitive, ignorant and ignorant population but the Chinese who they defeated did not. At the time that Genghis conquered the region in the year 1700, the people of Cathay were already a culture that was centuries old. They were awe-inspiring artists, musicians, poets as well as novelists and sculptors. They were already mastering techniques for printing which was unheard of throughout the world. They were experts in math, agriculture technology, astronomy and even architecture. They created the most stunning porcelains of the world. Their cooking was created to be a masterpiece. They had only just scratched the surface of their achievements. The entire way of life was one of perfection and grace, which was backed up by an ideology.

It was from this cultural world that the primitive Mongolians were introduced. They were in the traditions of Cathay and could not be able to resist the culture. They quickly became an integral part of the community of the people around them. They did not just become part of the tradition, but they also embraced it.

Chapter 8: Spring Hunting

The custom was for the Khan to live for the entire year in Cambalu and three months in spring during the great hunt as well as the summer months, June and July--in Xanadu.

In February, when the celebration of New Year's Eve was completed The Khan was ready for his spring hunt. After six months of winter at the Palace in Cambalu the Khan was a bit agitated. Each year during the spring, the Khan and his entourage were off on hunt.

Marco Polo was able to detail these hunts in a full detail since Marco Polo was frequently invited to go with the Khan.

Every year, at the beginning of March, Khan and his entourage quit their city Cambalu. The group usually headed to the ocean, as the land was heavily wooded and abounding in different kinds of wild animals.

The party that hunted included hundreds of guests, ladies in the royal court chiefs of the hunt, soldiers and even servants.

A wagon train that was long and full of food, tents and all else needed to ensure the safety of Khan and his family, began its journey first. After arriving at the spot in which the hunt was scheduled to take place, a variety of camp sites were constructed in various spots. The purpose was to ensure that hunters could be spread over the entire area. Naturally, the Khan's camp was the biggest.

A few hours after the train that provided food had left and the royal hunting group went to Cambalu. The Khan was riding on an elephant. The howdah was covered with gold-colored cloth and lined on the exterior by tiger skins Khan lay on the couch. The princes, along with the other guests of the royal court rode exquisite horses. Ladies of the court were transported in palanquins as were many servants. They were also watched by a select group of soldiers.

This group travelled with hunters who were skilled handlers of hunter dogs. Additionally, there were many falconers taking control of hunter falcons, hawks and the eagles. The birds, which belonged to Khan and his guests, were fastened on their legs silver rings on which were inscribed the names of their owners. The Khan also owned several well-trained animals like tigers, leopards and lynxes who, at certain times, were allowed to roam free in order to catch and retrieve wild animals from forests. The animals were utilized to hunt boars, wild oxen, animals like stags, bears and asses. They were transported by cages that were placed on wagons.

A few of Khan's most favored barons and ministers had specific duties while hunting. So, one baron could be in control of the equipment, and another was in charge of all the beaters used by hunters. Yet one would take care of another aspect of the game.

One baron Marco believed, was in an extremely odd job. He was referred to as"the "Keeper of Lost Property". If something was found, a cap, a piece clothes or even a falcon that was straying, it must be given to the baron. In the event of a failure to turn it over, it was regarded as theft and penalized. It was the obligation of the baron to ensure that the property forfeited returned to the rightful owner. As the tents were set up and the tents were put up, that of this baron was set on a high point and marked with flags that were distinctive to ensure that everyone could view. This way, Marco Polo observed, nothing could be lost, except that the tent was quickly repaired.

When he was on his way to Cambalu the Khan preferred to travel with a slower speed. On his horse, he often carried twelve falcons. For fun occasionally he would released a few to observe what bird they could track and then capture. This gave the Khan the greatest pleasure while lying on his couch and watched the falcons take on cranes, or other game birds.

Through these reroutes along the highway, the hours passed fast, and in the evening the Khan along with his entourage began to make their way for an area to camp. It was a huge camp of tents that was carefully placed around the huge camp of the Khan.

Tents of Khan were vast that it could easily accommodate huge crowds. The entrance was facing south. On the opposite side, there was another tent attached to it. It was a smaller tent that Khan employed for his private home. In at the rear to this tent, was an additional tent, in which his bed was. In close proximity were additional tents to accommodate the various parts of his family.

The Khan's tents were connected by silken cords and supported by pillars made of spice wood that were beautifully cut and gold-plated. The outsides of the tents were covered in skins from tigers while their interiors covered with the skins made of the sables and ermines. Sable skins were the most expensive and prized from the Mongols. Marco Polo said that a cloth made of sable skins was valued at two thousand dollars of gold.

In the vicinity of Khan's tent located the tents of court women, and those who were part of his household like his doctors and his astronomers.

On certain days, the Khan and his crew were hunting along the shores of lakes and rivers. They took birds like storks, swans and herons as well as other bird species. Other days, they hunted across the broad country alongside the Khan's experienced lynxes, tigers and leopards. On other days, the Khan's hunters hunted deep in the forest.

In hunting wild animals in the forests, the Khan used beaters to hunt wild animals. They wore staves with whistles formed a large circle that sometimes covered all of a mountain. When they received a signal, they started moving forward striking the bush with their stokes which drove every animal that came in front of them. When they moved forward, their circle swelled, making it nearly impossible for any animal to get through. Then, once the circle had swelled into one field and the entire wildlife all in one place The hunters were on the scene. Armed with bows, arrows, and spears, hunters came into the enclosure, and killed any animals that were trapped.

The various ways Khan and his guests in these various ways Khan and his guests entertain their guests while they went on the hunt in spring. The hunt lasted for three months. After this was up, all the party was re-introduced to Cambalu.

IN XANADU

" Five miles twice" of fertile land

The towers and walls were covered with girdles "

IT WAS

The custom followed by the Khan upon returning from hunting, was to stay for only three days in Cambalu. Then, at the conclusion of this time, all the court, as well as the Khan's thousands of white horses, retreated to Xanadu to the cooler Manchurian Hills, to spend during the scorching summer months.

On the day of celebration, an impressive procession was organized. The Khan riding a white horse led the way. On his exquisite horses, sat his sons, high-ministers and generals along with his favorite court guests, which included the trio of Polos. His Christian bodyguards accompanied the cavalcade.

Then came the countless palanquins, including the empresses and gorgeous ladies from the court. Then, they rolled out a seemingly interminable list of supply wagons, stewards and servants and court retainers. The countless white horses of

Khan, careful protected by special guards were also part of this parade.

From Cambalu towards Xanadu the road travelled through Xanadu in a direction north for one hundred and 18 miles. It crossed the Great Wall which separated Cathay from the plains of Mongolia. Plains in Mongolia.

When the Khan was out in his hunt for spring, a group of laborers, supervised by engineers and captains were dispatched to restore this highway and the numerous bridges it crosses to protect them from the damage caused by frosty winter nights. They also ensured that all the rest stops and campsites on the route were brought in good order and prepared to welcome the Khan as well as his court.

A few days prior to the day when the procession of Khan was scheduled set to begin at Cambalu the palace, a group of staff and groups of Khan's soldiers rode on the highway. The servants were responsible for the camps, while the army of Khan were stationed all over the road, notably at the intersections. The royal procession was been guarded, and no person was permitted to travel onto the highway when the Khan and his entourage traveling.

The royal procession marched in a steady pace for hours after hours. At the end of the afternoon, one the various royal camp locations was accessed and the entire group retreated to lay down in the evening. They found food, and everything else they needed in the waiting room. Then, after a break, participants of the court entertained themselves by taking part in archery competitions or wrestling as well as horse racing till the end of the night.

Every morning, the procession set at the same time. This way each day the courts travelled towards Xanadu.

As the procession approached at the Great Wall of China, that separated the country in Cathay from Mongolia and Mongolia, Khan called for a stop. He climbed up to the summit of the wall, and while in anticipation of the gathering and poured a sacred mare's milk from the golden goblet onto the Mongolian land. Mongolia. When he was done, the priest read a prayer to the land of his birth. After this sacred ceremony ended, the procession carried on along its route. Then, finally it took many days of travel, it arrived at Xanadu.

In the sun's spring light Xanadu glittered as a jewel crown. Khan built the beautiful summer palaces on the bank of the blue loan. Loan. The valley's marshland was drained, and formed into several lakes and islands and were linked by a series of curving waterways as well as arch-shaped stone bridges. The entire valley was turned into a huge park, dotted that was filled with stunning trees, beautiful flowering trees and lovely gardens. The area was filled by pagodas of various colors. The roofs that were upturned and topped with peaked of colored glazed tiles shimmered when the sun was shining on them. The pleasure boats swam idly through the rivers and lakes, with herons, swans cranes, as well as other water birds were seen lingering.

This is where in Xanadu the Khan constructed pleasure palaces made of marble, with wide connecting terraces. Teahouses in the garden were situated in long, sloping lawns which stretched to the shores of rivers. In a dazzling setting amid all the splendour was the grand palace of Khan. This palace in summer was built out of polished bamboo and embellished with gold carvings, and brilliant lacquers. Many of its rooms were embellished with vermilion and gold. Some of the walls were painted beautifully with birds, figures as well as distant landscapes.

The palaces behind them stretched out wide meadows, with stables that were long for horses as well as barracks for soldiers. There was also racing track where Khan's horses would race to entertain the court.

When he was settled on the Mongolian soil and inhaling the cool, fresh in the air of the mountains The Khan fell asleep and was at peace. He felt content. His mood was happy. Khan was felt across the court. In Xanadu the formalities were a bit less and during the scorching summer months, the majority of the courtly etiquette was left out.

All, males and women, had fun. The pool was a popular place to swim and frequently rode their bikes to the hills surrounding them. The group went to picnics, and played games.

In the indoors, they entertained themselves with entertainers, dancers as well as comedians, and the Yellow Lamas that created enthralling illusions. At the close of the season, a small group of Khan's Imperial Theatre was expected to arrive at Xanadu. Every year new shows and old classics were performed.

After the scorching summer months ended The Khan arranged an afternoon for his court to begin returning towards Cambalu. Cambalu. At the close of summer, the Khan was enjoying enough enjoyment and was now ready to begin the task of governing his vast empire. Every year in the final week in August, the lengthy royal procession began again along the road that connected Xanadu to Cambalu.

It's impossible to talk about Xanadu without mentioning a particular event that occurred in England just five centuries later Marco Polo had visited this tourist destination. After having read Marco Polo's tales and adventures, the famous poet Coleridge intrigued by Xanadu had a dream about the palaces that were the delight that belonged to the Khan. After waking, he sketched about what he'd seen during his nighttime dream. The poem, titled Kubla Khan, couldn't write out completely. The fragment could be reconstructed from his dream is revered in the present as one of most famous poems written in the world.

These are the enchanting words that start this famous, unfinished poem that was inspired by Marco Polo.

In Xanadu did Kubla Khan

The decree of the state-wide pleasure-dome:

The place where Alph The sacred river that runs through the area, was

In caverns that are unimaginable to the

A sunless ocean descends.

Also, twice five miles of fertile soil

Towers and walls covered with girdles:

There were also gardens that sparkled with the sexy rills

Incense was the most fragrant tree

There were also forests as old just like the hills.

Incorporating sunny green spots.

It's a huge loss for literature that this work isn't finished. It is also a huge loss for humanity that today, no remains of Xanadu is found. What's happened to the place of paradise that was created by Kublai?

Alas! The whole thing has fallen to pieces. The name itself, Xanadu, is hard to locate in a map, since it is the Chinese today call the location Shangtu.

The site is now empty, solitary site covered in rank weeds and grass. The valley has reverted to swampland. In the slope, where the beautiful castles built by the Khan used to be, just rubble and rock are visible. There and here, the outline of some walls of the foundation can be seen through the wreckage. On the ground, scattered are discarded pieces of white marble, stones of stone lions the carved dragons as well as other art pieces. All that is left of the old glory of Xanadu.

In the course of time, neglect and time has brought ruin and dust to what was once a place with splendour.

Chapter 9: Marco Polo Speaks Out

RETURNING from XANADU in the fall, Marco discovered Cambalu, the capital city. Cambalu in a state of military laws. One of Khan's highest ministers, who was known as Achmath was just killed. Security forces patrolled the streets, and anyone suspected of being involved was detained.

The Khan was angry. Achmath was among his most beloved characters and he promptly made judges responsible for deciding who was who were involved in the murder.

The Khan was, however, not realize that Achmath was untruthful. Achmath was the head of a gang of public officials who were able to make a lot of money by extortion and misappropriation.

Over the course of time, Achmath achieved great power over Khan with flattery and lies. Achmath always seemed to be dedicating his life entirely to serving the Khan but in truth Achmath was merely serving the interests of his own.

As time passed, his influence over the Khan grew too powerful that, in season of summer he returned to Cambalu and was appointed governor. He also received the power of dispersing posts in the government. They, naturally, were given to his friends and coworkers. A lot of them were governors, and were generally corruption-prone. Achmath, for every appointment, received an amount, in private, of dollars. He eventually gained a lot of money and had a beautiful residence located on one of the vast avenues in Cambalu. The man explained his riches with the claim that his wife had inherited huge property from her father as well as uncles.

In the event that anyone did protest, Achmath would take them before the

Khan and declare: "so-and-so has committed an offence against your dignity and deserves death". In return, the Khan who was awed by Achmath and Achmath, would reply: "do with so-and-so as you think right." So Achmath could remove his foes. This way, he attracted the attention of everyone and within a short time, nobody dared challenge him in any way. Nobody was such a high-ranking or strength that they could escape the fear of his.

He was now been killed with an assassin. Then Marco Polo was ordered by the Khan to study all reports in connection with the plan. He had to determine the reason why this crime was carried out.

As a result, Marco went to the royal dungeon, where he spoke to Chenchu, the murderer. Chenchu. Chenchu was Chenchu was a renowned Chinese military official. His lips Marco was able to understand what the motive behind the assassination and also the way it was carried out.

Chenchu spoke to Marco that he, along with another Chinese officer known as Vanchu were of the opinion Achmath's role in causing many unhappiness within the country of Cathay. In the end, they decided he had to be killed. They announced their decision to a large number of prominent citizens from every part of the country. A lot of them joined in the scheme. Achmath's murder was intended to start a massive rebellion in the face of Mongolian conquerors. Governors from all cities in Cathay were set to be killed.

"The Khan does not know how oppressed are the people of Cathay," Chenchu said. Chenchu. "You can see that the Khan of Cathay is an excellent ruler however he's not been able to ascend to the crown of

Cathay via hereditary right. He is a ruler by the process of conquest. We are conquered by the Khan. Also, the Khan is not confident in us. Therefore, he puts all the government power in the hands of Mongolians, Mohammedans and Christians. The majority of them were chosen by Achmath, the dictator. The people from Cathay are considered to be to be foreigners and would not wish to be oppressed by these men. Sometimes, they treat us as slaves. The most tyranted in all of them could be Achmath."

After that, Chenchu shared a long tale of the sexism which Achmath and his associates committed against the population. Then he told Marco that Vanchu and Vanchu upon entering the palace's rooms, sent an official to the residence of Achmath, the corrupt minister. Achmath in order to inform him that the crown prince Prince Chinkin who was the oldest child of the Khan was returning to Cambalu and wanted to meet the prince immediately. It was, in fact, was an untruth.

While waiting, Vanchu donned an opulent robe and pretend that he was Chinkin. After lighting a number of tallow candles, Vanchu waited patiently for the chief. Chenchu was secluded in a robe, with a powerful sword.

When Achmath was able to pass through the palace's gates wall, the guardsman of the guard was concerned.

"Where are you bound for at this late hour?" He demanded.

"To the Crown Prince Chinkin, who has just arrived," said the minister.

"How can that be?" replied the guard captain. "I didn't hear about his appearance. These are things I ought to be aware of. I'd better be together with you."

A few soldiers moved a short distance in the direction of Achmath.

"As Achmath entered the chamber," Chenchu explained, Chenchu, "he saw many candles lit. Naturally, he thought the Crown Prince was in town because who else could have such a lavish appearance? Although he was unable to be able to see his face, he bows before the royal model. As he did I stepped out of hiding and quickly pulled out my sword and cut off his head. The moment I struck, the captain and his men were in the room. As they watched the head fall towards the ground and recognizing Vanchu wearing a royal dress and robes, the captain aimed an arrow swiftly at the heart of Vanchu. Vanchu fell dead. The soldiers took me over and made me a prisoner. It was exactly as it happened," concluded Chenchu.

"And the other cities of Cathay, why did they not revolt against their governors?" inquires Marco.

"Had our mission been a success, they'd have felt a sense of pride. However, with Vanchu killed, me detained and accused of the crime of treason, and martial law being declared in the town of Cambalu They did not have the courage to stand up... I now await my end. The things I've done, I did for the citizens who live in Cathay."

Following Marco Polo had heard this tale and had gathered all the information pertaining to the attempted rebellion as possible, he took it into the Khan. He swore out loudly even though he was aware that his remarks against Achmath, the former minister Achmath was not going to please the Khan.

The man told the Khan precisely what he'd learned about corruption in Achmath and how, for the past 22 years, he was committing unending tyranny against the inhabitants who lived in the area. Marco told the Khan that he had sold his public offices, and also how he was paid commissions from every tax collectors. "All his wealth came from dishonesties," Marco stated. "Call in his sons and have them examined; then you will know that I speak the truth."

The boys were taken before the Khan and readily admitted that their father gained his fortune through dishonest ways. As the boys also admitted that they'd aided their father by requesting exorbitant payments and graft in exchange for money, the Khan demanded that they be beat by canes. Once this was accomplished, and the canes were removed, he ordered the whole treasure accumulated by his minister should be taken.

For the captain Chenchu along with the other members involved in the plan, they were ordered to be executed.

The Khan was awed by everything Marco Polo related and he made sure that justice was served. He was able to remove the Achmath family's friends Achmath from the office and appointed governors to be instructed to exercise justice and to abide by the legal limits.

Once the entire affair had been completed, when the entire affair was over, Khan was able to call Marco Polo before the throne In the presence of his ministers, he thanked Marco Polo for his bravery to stand up for what he believed in. He also appointed him an assessor of his privy council. In front of the entire council in attendance, he handed him the formal robes for this prestigious post and also a gold tablet of power.

Then Marco bows to the ground four times after accepting the gift and pledged that he would be loyal to Khan. Khan.

PRINTING, ICE-CHARCOAL AND ASTROLOGERS

A HIGH-RANKING official of the Khan's council of privy, Marco was informed about the structure of the federal government.

In order to carry the weight of administration, Khan established two high courts. One of them was a body for military named the Thai. The second entity, that was responsible for civilian activities, was called the Sing. Each tribunal was housed in a separate facility that was its own.

The Thai tribunal was the most powerful army body in Thailand and was accountable only for the Khan. It was comprised of 12 high-ranking nobles who were in charge of every aspect of military affairs. They were the ones who approved troop movements as well as the strategies for every military campaign.

The Sing tribunal was responsible for all internal affairs for the provinces comprising the thirty-four regions of the nation. It also included twelve people. The tribunal was sometimes referred to as the second tribunal due to the fact that it was not regarded to be as significant as the military tribunal.

In the Sing structure, each province of the country had its own office wing. In the Sing building, there were departments for taxation and justice, as well as highways, trade and currency.

However, Marco Polo was not only concerned about the structure of the Khan's administration, but he was also fascinated by the inhabitants he observed within and in and around Cambalu. He was fascinated by the way they lived their lives and worked. He found many aspects that were not common within Europe.

In addition to that, Marco saw in Cambalu the printing process using moving type. This technique wasn't widely recognized in Europe until about two hundred years after. The man also noticed another aspect which he believed to be the most remarkable. They made use of black stones as energy rather than wood! The stone, which was mined in mountains, was transported to the city. Then, Marco noticed that it was burning as charcoal, and it was superior to wood because it could easily sustain the flame until dawn. It also released a large amount of energy.

Even though it was a rarity in Europe in the time of this coal was not even a thing but in Cathay it was employed as a fuel since early time. It was referred to as "ice charcoal".

Marco was told that across the region of Cathay the inhabitants were agnostic. It was believed by the constellations on the night sky had an impact on our lives and also predicted certain future events. In accordance with the location of the celestial bodies, it was possible to predict what days were fortunate and also which ones were unlucky.